STRAIGHT*FORWARD*

Ways to Live & Lead

PAM IORIO

Former Mayor of Tampa, Florida

To Keith with best
wishes for success –

Pam
2018

To my family—the best part of my life.
My husband, Mark
Our children, Caitlin and Graham
My mother, Dorothy
And in memory of my father, John

TABLE OF CONTENTS

—◈◈◈—

ACKNOWLEDGMENTS

—⟨✑⟩—

I APPRECIATE ALL OF THE assistance I received in writing this book. My husband, Mark Woodard, was my sounding board, editor and support throughout the entire process. I could not have written the book without him. Our children, Caitlin and Graham, gave excellent advice and caused me to think in different ways. From the start, Fran Davin provided guidance and structure, helping with overall organization, themes and editing. My brother, Jay Iorio, imparted valuable ideas. I am indebted to Karen Post for her straightforward advice and Ellen Schneid Coleman for her superior editing. Suzanne Brownstein helped me navigate the publishing world. Don and Kathy Wyly made sure my father would have been satisfied with the final manuscript. I am grateful to friends who took the time to edit various drafts and improved the final product immensely: Kalyn Brandewie, Kasey Kelly, Roger and Elizabeth Kurz, Liana Lopez, Linda Marcelli, and Elaine Shimberg. They have all been generous with their time and talent.

Introduction

*"If your actions inspire others to dream more, learn more,
do more and become more, you are a leader."*

John Quincy Adams

WE HAVE A LEADERSHIP PROBLEM in our country. It's not confined to one party or ideology. The void exists in much of our political and corporate worlds. We are a great country, but our leaders are falling short. It is perhaps the single most important threat to our democracy and our competitiveness in the global economy. This lack of leadership on the political front, a result of both parties being entrenched in ideological struggles, keeps the nation from moving forward. When acquiring power becomes the ultimate goal, solutions to the country's problems take a back seat. The middle ground, where so many answers can be found, is a casualty.

On the corporate front, nothing speaks louder about the lack of leadership than the financial crisis that began in 2008. Wall Street company executives who relied on a financial bailout from the taxpayers showed neither remorse nor shame over their single-minded concern for profits that drove our nation to the brink of economic collapse.

How do we address this serious problem? By developing leaders who embrace what I call a straightforward style. My three decades in public life have convinced me that you can be an exemplary leader in whatever field you choose, but it takes effort, commitment, and discipline.

In this book, I examine the qualities, traits, characteristics, and competencies of the straightforward leader. It is for the individual who is ready to improve his leadership abilities, achieve more, and, in turn, help organizations and others around him reach their full potential.

Straightforward leadership is a style that is distinctively direct, clear, honest, strategic, and respectful. It provides room for compromise and seeks to bring people together instead of dividing them. This brand of leadership is pragmatic, not ideological; solution based and results oriented. It recognizes the importance of ongoing growth, learning, and change.

This book is about the components of straightforward leadership, the inner leadership qualities that are essential to being a role model for others, and the importance of substance and credibility. I describe how crisis and tragedy come into our lives and how straightforward leaders find a way to lead themselves and others during difficult times. I highlight the new reality of our rapidly changing world and how the true leader embraces innovation and brings others along as partners. The importance of a centered life is underscored—how you must lead yourself well before you can lead others. This book describes the leader who has acquired impressive qualities and competencies that cause others to look to him for guidance.

Almost everyone has the capacity for leadership. A few people may be "born leaders," but they are the exception, not the rule. For most of us, leadership qualities are developed over time. In my case, effective leadership traits were formed over three decades of public service, the last eight as mayor of the city of Tampa. Elected to the County Commission in Hillsborough County at the age of 26, I was in a public and demanding role early in my career. Leadership lessons came rapidly. A positive mentor early in my career, trial and error, marriage, and parenthood all helped me see better ways to live and lead. My career path led me to become the county's Supervisor of Elections where, as luck would have it, I served during the tumultuous 2000 presidential election in Florida and learned valuable leadership lessons that served me well in guiding statewide election reform.

In 2003, I became mayor of Tampa, the nation's fifty-fourth largest city. After two terms[1] of successfully steering the city, first through boom years, and, later, the Great Recession, I gained insight into how to manage crisis and lead a large and complex organization through change.

Tampa is a microcosm of America and reflects our country in the twenty-first century. Diverse culturally and racially, Tampa is a big city with a small town nature that welcomes newcomers. It is home to many budding entrepreneurs and a community of tightly knit neighborhoods. Tampa's financial, social, and economic challenges are shared by most communities across our country. We hosted four Super Bowls and landed the Republican National Convention in 2012. As the center of commerce for the west coast of Florida, it is home to an acclaimed international airport, a bustling port, a major air force base, and outstanding academic institutions. With a budget of nearly $800 million and 4,500 employees, the city serves not only its residents, but also the thousands of visitors and commuters that arrive everyday.

---

1. Tampa's term limit law prevented me from running again.

My straightforward leadership style produced results. Crime was reduced by 61.5 percent—far more than the state and national trend. The downtown waterfront was radically transformed to house two beautiful museums and a spectacular park. The waterfront was opened to the people with the construction of the Tampa Riverwalk, ultimately a 2.2 mile urban path along our river connecting downtown amenities. Despite the deep recession, and decline in virtually every city revenue source, cash reserves tripled from $50 million to $150 million. Residential living finally became a reality in the downtown with over $1 billion in private investment. Historically neglected areas of the city thrived with a focused plan of revitalization. Integrity became the foundation for how my administration served the public. Looking back I see how our careful plans turned to successful governance. Years of straightforward leadership made a difference.

My career in public service has been grounded in my love of this great country. Throughout the book, I note times in our history that provide inspiration for today. History is a useful leadership guide for it reminds us that we have collectively faced obstacles, adversity and calamity, and have emerged stronger. I often think back to our revolutionary war era and the fight for independence, a part of our history that brought out the best in leadership. Understanding the past and its lessons gives me confidence to face today's challenges.

We occupy a special place in the world—a beacon of hope for people seeking freedom and opportunity. We have earned a reputation as a world leader and with that status comes an expectation, an obligation to lead. We should always strive to be leaders on the world stage as innovators, thinkers, entrepreneurs and humanists. We owe it to those who have come before us to continue their high standards of achievement and provide quality leadership in all that we undertake.

The path to straightforward leadership is the substance of this book. Each chapter is designed to help you understand the essential elements of this style of leadership so you can:

- *Develop your inner leadership qualities:* We begin by examining the qualities that are essential for the exceptional leader. Honesty and humility, a positive attitude, a measured and thoughtful approach, the ability to admit mistakes and accept responsibility, competing without excuses, resiliency, showing respect for others, and the careful use of power. One of the fundamental keys to leadership is understanding that it starts with you.

- *Become a person of substance:* People gravitate towards those with knowledge and expertise. It is critical for leaders to build a body of knowledge that makes them credible and to find positive mentors who can guide their growth, hire people with skill sets that exceed their own, and keep learning no matter how long you have been in the job.

- *Manage crisis and tragedy:* My years as mayor were scarred by the terrible loss of four police officers killed in the line of duty. Regardless of your title or position, you are not immune to loss and emotional lows. Nevertheless, a leader must muster the strength to perform. Learn what steps you can take to effectively manage crisis and tragedy.

- *Become a change leader:* Change has changed. The status quo is no longer an option in our fast changing world. Leaders must be in the forefront of setting the tone and a catalyst for positive transformation. See how strategic planning helps make change easier, the importance of choosing your change battles, and the necessity of embracing technological advances.

- *Live a centered life:* Leadership begins with how you lead yourself. A leader has two lives, the personal and the professional, separate, yet congruent and supportive of each other. A straightforward leader must be well grounded. This chapter describes the traits and habits of a focused, well-rounded and caring person, the leader who possesses the confidence to take risks and try new things. We look at the importance of creating a balance between the home and work.

These five areas capture the basics of straightforward leadership. We are all a work in progress and it would be difficult to find someone who excels in all of these things. Introspection brings clarity and improvement. As you develop into an exceptional leader, you will also broaden yourself into a better person, one capable of putting the needs of others first and helping those around you grow and change.

Read and reflect on how you can become the straightforward leader that is sorely needed by our society today. There are organizations that need improvement, problems to be solved, change that needs to be implemented. Our world should be about forward progress, new ideas, and tackling the tough issues. It takes real leadership, and that leadership begins with you.

Chapter One

—⟡—

DEVELOP YOUR INNER LEADERSHIP QUALITIES

THERE ARE STRIKING SIMILARITIES AMONG people who are straightforward, effective leaders. From the vantage point of three decades in public life, I've observed leaders in the worlds of business, government, military, and non-profits. Working with them, it became clear to me that no matter the field, we all have within us *the ability* to grow as a leader, but not all of us take advantage of it. If you want to lead, the first step is to understand the traits and characteristics an outstanding leader must have, and what you must to do to call those qualities your own.

In this chapter I describe those qualities and show you how you can develop the inner leadership characteristics that make you capable of long-term achievement. The most important qualities any leader can develop are:

- Honesty and humility
- A positive and optimistic attitude

- The ability to make measured and thoughtful decisions
- The ability to admit mistakes and accept responsibility
- The ability to compete—win or lose—without making excuses
- Resilience
- Respect and kindness
- The ability to use power carefully

You can't get to work on developing these important qualities until you perform one very important action—to honestly evaluate yourself and your shortcomings. The path to better leadership must be paved with absolute humility. Before you can achieve your goal, you have to first recognize that you do not yet possess all that it takes to be a great leader.

Here then is the path:

1. Recognize the traits and characteristics to straightforward leadership,
2. Evaluate your own strengths and weaknesses with complete honesty, and, finally,
3. Acknowledge that you must consciously develop these inner leadership qualities.

We are all works in progress and from time to time even the best leaders fall short in meeting every expectation they and others have of them. It takes a great deal of discipline to go through this evaluation process, and then to commit to continually work to improve yourself both professionally and personally.

A true leader aspires to master these qualities that lead to long term achievement.

Honesty and Humility

If you ask any person on the street "Are you honest?" their answer will likely be an emphatic, "Of course!" People are quick to answer, it's almost reflexive. Consider this: What if you asked the same person this question instead—"Are you honest with yourself?" The person might pause.

That's the real test of honesty. It involves a certain amount of self-analysis and introspection as well as a heavy dose of humility. All of us are imperfect and a truly honest evaluation reveals faults and weaknesses and parts of our personalities we'd rather not confront. Humility requires that we recognize our imperfections. Honesty demands a conscious effort to change and make yourself better. Both are essential traits of a straightforward leader.

Straightforward leadership starts with being honest about yourself. As you read this chapter, which examines each of these leadership traits, you will realize that each of them entails a completely candid conversation with yourself to determine to what extent you already have developed these inner qualities and where you need improvement. From there, it takes persistent work and ongoing self-evaluation.

If you are completely satisfied with yourself, this approach won't work. How often do you hear someone say, "I am what I am," and that's pretty much the end of their self-analysis and attempt to improve. Many in positions of leadership are content bringing their personality—their good and bad traits—to work. They may not even realize they have "bad" traits, that is, traits that detract from rather than enhance their ability to lead. They lack introspection and have no desire to change. They are not honest with themselves.

"Honesty first."

A new role with new responsibilities requires different behaviors and approaches. I have witnessed newly elected public officials

3

fail miserably as leaders because they lack the honesty to assess their shortcomings, learn from others, and change the way they do business. Ego gets in the way, particularly coming off the high of getting elected. The last thing most people want to embark on is a course in self-improvement when a majority of the electorate has just elevated them to a position of authority.

The same is true in corporate life. Promotions don't always mean the person has developed the requisite inner leadership qualities. The result is the person has a title that does not necessarily reflect their true ability to lead. When people are placed in a high leadership position, yet won't honestly confront their own truths, their lack of grounding and self-confidence makes them defensive and short-tempered. Such leaders typically become secretive and surround themselves with a coterie in the organization they feel are loyal to them.

In my experience, the best leaders are those who are humble and self-effacing, often using self-deprecating humor to make a point. They realize they are a work in progress. They always want to be a little bit better than they were the day before.

Honesty begins with you. Only then can you bring this all-important quality to your organization.

"Truth is the glue," said Gerald Ford after assuming the presidency following the scandal-ridden tenure of President Richard Nixon. In the wake of Watergate and the public's shattered confidence in the integrity of the nation's top leader, Ford's declaration was simply stated, correct, and hence reassured Americans that he would be truthful with them. We want the same truthfulness not only from our leaders in government but from those in business, non-profits, or any other group in which we participate. Honesty defines you as a person and distinguishes your organization. Your organization will thrive when people know that the leader has been honest with himself, and now brings that strong ethical foundation to the entire team. Simply put, *a person without an ethical core cannot be a viable leader.*

> "Truth is the glue."

On election night in 1985, when I was first elected to the county commission, my mentor and campaign manager Fran Davin looked at me and said, "Don't ever take a dive."

She meant don't ever walk away from an issue, and don't ever do something you don't believe in. I have always followed these simple rules.

Public service is an honor, a way to express appreciation for your American citizenship. Our Founding Fathers saw public service as a pure form of representation, thus free from tyranny and oppression. To work, democracy depends on honesty, openness, and an understanding of what it means to be a public "servant." You cannot think of yourself as better than the people you serve or seek special treatment. Similarly, the act of operating a business in America is an affirmation of the free market system that has built our country and has provided a high standard of living for many. Those operating businesses — from the community banker to the neighborhood deli owner — should consider themselves to be in a position of honor and trust.

When I became mayor, my staff and I not only developed strategic goals but also defined the values of the organization. These values could be applied to any organization: integrity, excellence, teamwork, and respect. We stated them and restated them so that all employees understood the standards of conduct expected.

When I left office after eight years, I looked with pride at my staff. Never once in eight years had there been a question raised as to their integrity. No business deal that favored a particular individual. No ill will created in the community. No actions that in any way cast a shadow over city government. They were all people of the highest integrity and it showed.

Nothing will sap the energy from an organization faster than the lack of attention to high standards, fair treatment, and honesty. People can understand the lack of a pay increase or a temporary suspension to a retirement plan, but to keep an employee at his job when he has committed an ethical breach — that is the real morale killer. Employees want to be proud of where they work and that sense of pride comes from the ethical climate.

Honesty and humility are the cornerstone of straightforward leadership.

A Positive Attitude

A friend of mine is a corporate CEO who has steadily grown his organization by double digits every year. Recently over lunch we discussed a complex merger plan that he had been working on for months that had fallen through. As you can imagine, a lot of time, effort, and money had been devoted to this promising business transaction. Even though the deal fell through, you would have thought my friend had just found oil under his company's land. Upbeat and positive, he discussed all the good that had come from the discussions and how much he and the others in his company had learned. He saw the experience in an affirmative light because that's how he views life. Seeing the world in a positive, optimistic way is a key component of a straightforward leader.

If you assembled the top fifty business leaders in the country, you wouldn't find a pessimist among them. Why? Because successful leaders see opportunities to improve, expand, and grow their organizations. Their optimism attracts and inspires people and makes them feel good about the mission and the organization. They show a passion and pride in what they do that is contagious. They also find ways to control the quality of their day. While they recognize that many things that happen on any given day are outside of their control, they find ways to turn the negative to a positive. Being positive and optimistic isn't just about a cheery "good morning" at the office; it is the belief that you can take a day with all of its twists and turns, its good and bad news, and see in all of these experiences a path forward. It's about gratitude and appreciating what you have and enthusiastically acknowledging your reality.

Not long ago, I met with a friend who is a very successful broadcast journalist in the local market. She lamented that she couldn't convince her husband to have a second child. They have a beautiful daughter, fulfilling careers, and live in a lovely home. My friend had so much to be happy about, yet she was so unhappy that she reached out and sought my advice. I asked, "If you can't change your husband's mind, why not embrace what you do have? You have a lot!" This conversation caused her to think in a different way not only about this issue, but also about how she faced other issues in her life. Her attitude changed and she found renewed focus and pleasure in both her work and personal life.

Many times we make the mistake of thinking about what we don't have instead of being grateful for what we do have. Switching your perspective from dissatisfaction stemming from what you perceive you lack to appreciating and relishing what is good in your life can change the way you approach each day. Accepting reality can not only make your perspective more positive, it can become a catalyst for change.

Fundamentally, we have to believe that we control the quality of our day. Many of us do not realize the important role we all play in the kind of day we have; in fact, many of us abdicate control over the quality of our day to others. You can blame a host of factors for a bad day—your boss, your spouse, or the dry cleaner that ruined your favorite jacket.

Conversely, you might be the one making others unhappy (sadly, not everyone learns to control the quality of their day). Decide for yourself what kind of environment you want to create for yourself and those around you.

As mayor, I wanted to work with constructive, positive people who inspired others to do their best for the taxpayers. In my early months in office, I got to know all of the department directors from the previous administration. While most had many years of experience, I was looking for a combination of knowledge and a "can-do" attitude. Unfortunately, a "can't-do" attitude prevailed in some cases. One example says it all.

One evening during my first month in office I arrived home and my husband, Mark, informed me that a Mr. Bloch had called me. He jokingly added "Maybe it's H & R Block," the nationally known tax preparation firm. Turned out he was right; it was Richard Bloch of H & R Block, who wasn't very happy. In 1999, Mr. Bloch had executed an agreement accompanied by a gift of $1 million to construct a park that would provide inspiration to cancer survivors. Mr. Bloch, himself a cancer survivor, had been very generous with his gifts to build public spaces across the country as refuges for cancer survivors and their families. Though construction had started in 2000, it was now 2003 and he was not satisfied with what he saw. The project did not meet his original expectations, and his phone calls to city officials left him frustrated. "Mayor," he said exasperated, "they treat me like I'm a gnat on an elephant's behind!" I immediately looked into the situation and found inertia, finger-pointing, and inaction. We jump-started the project, making it a priority of a person I knew I could rely on to get the job done—my new chief of staff—someone I had brought with me from the Supervisor of Elections office. We got the rest of the funding in place, and finally completed the Richard and Annette Bloch Cancer Survivors Park. I knew then that the organization needed an infusion of positive energy—a different type of leadership.

We all have negative people in our lives. When I speak to groups on the subject of negativity in the workplace, it always provokes knowing laughter. In one speech I said in jest that it would be more productive for a company to pay the downers to stay home. A manager of a business came up to me and said, "Good idea, I may do just that!" People see negativity like a cancer. You put one gloomy person in an organization, and even if nine of the ten people are positive go-getters, that one person can drag the group down faster than anything else. People with a sour attitude are the last to see it in themselves. They lack the self-evaluation and introspection so key to being a leader. They are not honest with themselves.

As mayor, I surrounded myself with a positive team, which is one reason we accomplished so much. Early on I decided to control the quality of my day. A bad newspaper article. Get over it. A meeting that didn't go well. Look forward to the next meeting and fix what went wrong. The key is the ability to start each day fresh, unwounded by the slings and arrows from the day before. Adopting this attitude may sound easy, but doing it is not so simple. It is learned behavior and difficult to achieve. It takes a conscious and deliberate effort to take the hurts, the criticisms, and the meanness of the previous day and start the day anew. It has taken me decades to train myself to act in this way and even now I don't always succeed in immediately forgiving those whom I believe have been unkind or unfair. I try to remember Nelson Mandela's wise comment that, "forgiveness liberates the soul." If he can live his life that way after being unjustly imprisoned for 27 years, surely I can find a way to forgive someone for something far less important.

"Negativity is contagious."

Life is a series of peaks and valleys. The valleys are inevitable. Don't let them devastate you. Who among us hasn't experienced peaks, valleys, and everything in between? Approaching life in a positive way helps us handle the valleys.

For me, keeping an upbeat frame of mind meant making small changes in my life so I could feel good about the quality of each day. One thing that helped keep me sane was refusing to schedule anything other than the most critical city business on Sunday. I needed time to decompress and be with my family, do chores, and have a relaxing Sunday dinner. Staying thoughtful and on an even-keel requires time away from your position of responsibility. No matter what your career, you've got to carve out time that gives you a chance to think and replenish your energy.

It became a habit to come home for dinner before a banquet. Our family ate together and then I attended the evening function. I had no need to eat at a banquet anyway since the purpose was to network or conduct business. I felt better about being out for the evening when I knew our family had spent time together first. Little things like this contributed to keeping me enthusiastic about the next event, the next challenge, and so on. Because of term limits, I knew I only had a limited number of years as mayor to be productive and relevant to the progress of our community. For me to be at my best, my orientation had to be towards the positive, the good, and the art of the possible.

Being positive is an important element of straightforward leadership. You have achieved this when you consistently embrace reality, appreciate the good, and see the world as a place of possibilities.

Be Measured and Thoughtful

Leaders make decisions that can affect taxpayers, shareholders, employees, contributors, and their friends and family. Since your judgment has such significance, let time be your tool. Time aids in the decision-making process. If an issue is important and involves digesting a number of different facts or points of view, don't rush to judgment. Acquire more information. Think it through. A measured and thoughtful approach to decision-making is a hallmark of a straightforward leadership style.

A person may have a lot of experience or educational credentials, but the quality of their judgment is vital to the value they bring to an organization. As you grow in your leadership positions and assume greater responsibility within your organization, you are increasingly evaluated not only by your final decision but the manner in which you come to that conclusion. A final outcome may be outside of your control as other external factors may come into play but your thought process is within your control. *How you conduct yourself throughout the decision-making process is critical to straight-forward leadership.*

I have learned over the years to reach conclusions only after carefully weighing all sides and facts. This was not my style when I first started my public career, but years of experience have taught me the importance of thorough deliberation. Being measured and thoughtful should be reflected in all of your external communications from speeches to e-mails. Many times, particularly in my early years as mayor, something would happen and my staff and I would conclude that we had to respond with a letter from me stating the city's position.

As it turned out, the letter was usually unnecessary.

By the time a draft had been written, circulated among the staff for edits, and came back to my desk for signature, the problem had often resolved itself.

A lot of people dash off a letter or e-mail in anger or irritation; that's a mistake. Communications initiated in an emotional state are usually not businesslike and often inflame rather than resolve an issue. It is always best to take a 24-hour **"Don't overreact."** hour cooling off period. Sometimes what appears to be an issue in need of resolution turns out not to be an issue.

Answers are usually found in the middle. When I was first elected to the county commission, I was faced with rezoning and land use decisions every other week. How should a parcel of land be zoned and for what use? I quickly realized just how "gray" this area was—there were very few clear-cut black and white cases. Instead, decisions were gradations of gray based upon past and current uses, neighborhood feedback, or input from professional planners. Many judgments you make fall into the gray area; there is no real right or wrong. A thoughtful, measured approach to analyzing issues is crucial to a leader.

Straightforward leadership disappears when ideology trumps facts and thoughtfulness. This is a huge problem in government today. Pragmatic leadership requires honesty and humility, which allow you to thoughtfully consider all sides and be respectful of the other person's point of view. An important component of being measured and thoughtful is the ability to compromise.

An immediate challenge for me as mayor had to do with a proposed art museum to replace the existing outdated facility. My predecessor had plans for a 150,000-square-foot art museum that would reshape a major downtown block. The city had already borrowed money to build it, predicated on the private sector coming up with matching monies. In addition, a luxury condo was to be built on public waterfront park land adjacent to the museum.

From the beginning, I was dubious about the project. I was also troubled about the loss of public park land, which I believed needed to remain open to the public and provide access to the river. The condo plan didn't survive my first week in office.

The private sector, though they tried very hard, had not raised the necessary matching funds to start the project, and I was uneasy that they would not be able to raise the remaining matching funds for construction. I was even more concerned that the cost of operating and maintaining the museum would fall to the taxpayers. As for the museum, which had a very small endowment, no business plan existed to show how it would succeed financially. I was committed to protecting taxpayers from construction cost overruns and operating deficits. At that time, with the building industry booming, the anticipated cost for the museum kept rising. When the business plan was finally completed, it showed the museum running at a considerable deficit.

For two years I worked with members of the museum board who thought I was being a pain for not proceeding with the project. Finally, after much dialogue, when it became clear that the museum board was not going to be able to obtain the necessary bank loan, I put an end to the plan. That decision was controversial and disappointed the many advocates for a new museum. Though not everyone wanted the large 150,000-square-foot museum, most people did want a new museum to replace the aging facility. Many citizens who supported a new museum were concerned that the failure of the project meant we might never get a modern building.

Something had to be done. The old museum was in a bad state of repair, was architecturally uninspired, and sat in a drab park, which was unused although it was situated along our beautiful river waterfront. The entire area had a depressing quality; there was no life or vibrancy to the district.

Despite my opposition to the museum and condo plan, revitalizing our downtown and making Tampa a city of the arts were two of my administration's strategic goals; now we were able to use the opportunity to start over with our vision for downtown. The downtown needed a beautiful and lively waterfront park especially since the waterfront was barely used and represented a missed opportunity for our city. With the old museum plan off the table, we began a new dialogue about how the waterfront should develop. After much public debate and endless meetings with stakeholders, a decision was finally reached. It wasn't easy getting to a unified decision between the city and the art museum board, but, ultimately, we got past our irritation with one another and agreed to build a 66,000-square-foot museum at the edge of the newly revitalized park adjacent to the river. The city contracted with landscape architect Thomas Balsley to design a first-class waterfront park that would not only be the front lawn of the museum, but also a county-wide destination point for our downtown. Two years earlier I had arranged for the city to make land available at the corner of the park for a new children's museum and that project had moved forward. Our plan began to come together with the two museums sitting side by side with the Curtis Hixon Waterfront Park—with its playground, fountains, a great lawn, and dog park—as their front entryway.

The entire area is now a focal point of the city and has transformed our downtown. Once the park and the museums opened, the area became an instant gathering place. The park has won awards for its design and usability, and the public has embraced this new urban space enthusiastically. It is a good ending to what started as an unpleasant situation.

Today, if you stand in the Curtis Hixon Waterfront Park and look at the architecture of the two beautiful museums, you might not know that this represented an answer in the middle, a compromise. It appears visionary and expansive. It was a great compromise with many winners. One group did not trump another. The art museum patrons ended up with a first-rate museum that was smaller than the original design, but more affordable to operate. The city gained the art museum and a world-class children's museum, and the public won by getting added green space downtown and a beautifully designed park which is widely used. The public also won with an affordable art museum, which did not operate in the red, and access to the waterfront. Just focusing on a new art museum would have been tilting too far to one side of the equation without considering many other factors. The "right" answer for all constituents was in the middle.

Americans are in the middle on most things. They gravitate to the middle because, when the facts are distilled, that's where most of the answers are. We get ourselves into trouble when extreme views dominate the political parties who ultimately control problem-solving in our country. No wonder we have gridlock.

"Forge creative compromises."

Why has the notion of compromise been turned around today and made to seem as weakness? It takes great strength to take an idea you hold dear and decide to let part of it go. Our Founding Fathers led the way. Imagine the steamy summer of 1787 when the delegates to the Constitutional Convention met to try again to forge a union. The delegates in Philadelphia were divided on a host of critical issues. At least one struck at the very definition of a moral question: slavery. Think about this issue in the context of what we are arguing about today. Entitlements, tax loopholes, increase in revenues, spending cuts? Do any of these issues rise to the level of the debate over whether the new United States should abolish or allow slavery? In the end, they compromised, and although the compromise was imperfect, it gave this great experiment in democracy a chance to succeed.

Compromise is an outgrowth of a measured and thoughtful approach and is an integral part of straightforward leadership.

Being measured and thoughtful means you have to give yourself time to think. A new mayor, a new CEO, a new anything will be inundated. There are always people who are just waiting for the next person. Maybe they didn't get what they wanted from the last person in charge or have their own agenda they want to accomplish.

After my first six whirlwind months, I realized something critical was missing from my schedule: thinking time. Big decisions had to be made, but when was I thinking them through? A too-full schedule doesn't allow you thinking time. I didn't have enough time to reflect. Thereafter, we carved out time in my schedule for thinking. If you are in a position where you make major decisions, give yourself time to think. Block time out in your schedule so you are not moving frenetically from one meeting to another.

Decide how you are going to control the outline of each day so you can be the most productive. Take the clutter out of your life and focus on what's important. Giving yourself time to think and controlling your schedule so you can live in a rational, sane way are keys to success. I didn't learn this lesson until I became mayor. Once I did, it made me a better leader.

"Big decisions require undistracted time to reflect. Find the time."

Technology is a huge part of our lives. From the time we wake up and pick up our cell phones, check our e-mail messages, get on the Internet, read the news, and dive into our work, we are constantly multitasking. We have enormous work demands, and we still have to be on top of our personal lives. One close friend in local politics is always frazzled. He is tied to his phone, texting and Twittering even when he's talking with others. He wants to answer everyone's question or concern immediately. I worry about him! What he doesn't realize is that he is living on auto-pilot, answering people the moment a message reaches him. Where's the thoughtfulness that goes with being an effective leader?

As I said earlier, mastering each leadership quality requires a conscious and continual effort. Even the most measured and thoughtful leader can become exasperated and quick to judge at times. Compromise is not always easy to achieve. Some decisions are made based on emotion and not facts. Some seek perfection— it's not possible—and the result is stasis. Consistent thoughtfulness and a measured approach is a discipline that requires considerable effort.

Admit Mistakes, Accept Responsibility

There is a tremendous responsibility that comes with being a leader. You not only must take responsibility for your own actions, you also must assume responsibility for the mistakes members of your team or organization make.

In any organization a certain number of errors are bound to occur. They are a part of being human. I've made plenty. Think about mistakes you or your staff have made. Do you take responsibility for them, analyze the reasons for them, and learn from them? If your answer is "yes," it demonstrates a positive attitude and that, with each mistake, you are growing.

If you see only your strengths, your ego is out of control. If you see only your weaknesses, you'll become a basket case. Mistakes can help you see both your strengths and weaknesses and put them in perspective.

Sometimes you make a hiring error. In my first year as mayor I selected the wrong candidate for a high-ranking position. He was a good person and an excellent fit in his previous job, just not the right fit for the top job. Problems mounted. I coached and counseled him, but the problems did not go away. Finally, I knew a change was needed. When I analyzed what went wrong, I realized that when you have to ask someone to resign or fire them, it really means you made a misstep in the hiring process. It is your mistake, not the person's. As a leader, you must take responsibility and learn from it.

> "Only if you admit mistakes can you learn from them."

This is one area where boards of directors as well as top management of corporations and non-profits often need help. Boards hire but are reluctant to fire. Nobody wants to fire and hurt someone's career. But I have seen boards close their eyes to all sorts of transgressions at the top and ignore the problems rather than deal with them. One reason this occurs is that a board has to first admit they may not have hired the right person to begin with. Often board members grow close to the executive director or CEO who runs the organization and thus lose the ability to step back and objectively evaluate performance.

I once observed a troubled organization that had huge management and financial challenges. During a board meeting the long-time CEO seemed more like a spectator than the person in charge. He ultimately blamed the financial morass on the fact that the CFO position was vacant. Never did he take full responsibility for the problem. Board members should be wary of top officials who can't admit their mistakes and learn from them.

Boards share the blame when this occurs because they enable this sort of behavior by not holding the leader or themselves accountable. They make excuses for the CEO, and get emotional or sentimental about the great job the person has done in the past. Many boards forget their fiduciary responsibility. As leaders of an organization, board members must step up and assume responsibility if they have failed to act on financial, management, or behavior problems. In order to properly perform the role of a board member you first have to see your role as serious and recognize that it has consequences. Forget about what an honor it is to have been selected to serve on a particular board. Don't focus on your social and emotional ties to the staff. Read the financial statements and ask the questions that need to be asked. If there are transgressions, deal with them in an appropriate and professional manner. Don't abdicate responsibility to an organization by being passive, concerned with being well-liked, or afraid of upsetting the apple cart. I suspect that in retrospect a lot of directors of financial institutions wish they had asked more questions of management prior to the financial meltdown our country experienced in 2008.

Mistakes and responsibility go hand in hand. We live in a society where it is increasingly rare for a leader to accept responsibility for a mistake. My rule of thumb is that if leaders cannot readily accept responsibility for what's gone wrong, they don't deserve the title of leader. Period. I have seen over and over again executive directors of non-profits, high ranking government officials, and business executives pass the blame on to someone else in the organization. While it may be true that someone else made the error, the leader must bear the responsibility. Worse still are top leaders who blame their woes on the media. That is perhaps the biggest dodge of all. As a close observer of the media for three decades, I cannot recall an instance where *they* were responsible for problems of an agency, business, or government body. Reporting on a problem, often to the discomfort of the top leader or the board of directors, doesn't translate to causing a problem. Blaming the media is the ultimate deflection of responsibility and signals a lack of straightforward leadership at the helm.

I made quite a blunder the first time I had to cut positions at city hall. My first four years as mayor were during the boom years. Then, in 2007, the Florida Legislature implemented changes that caused all local governments to roll back property tax rates. It was an effort on the Legislature's part to deal with citizen outrage over property insurance costs. As is often the case in politics, issues get lumped together. The Legislature never did fix the property insurance problem that ignited the furor, but did manage to restrict local government revenue. This occurred the year *before* the bottom fell out of the economy, which required even more severe cuts in the ensuing years. This rollback in the property tax rate meant cuts, and since 80 percent of the city's budget was personnel—salaries and benefits—it meant that jobs had to be eliminated.

My staff and I were determined to be methodical. No cuts across the board. Judicious cuts in areas where we felt the public would not be adversely affected. Yet, in spite of what I thought was sensible planning, I started what became four years of cutting and saving by making a significant miscalculation in my approach: I set a date on which all of the layoffs would occur.

I held a press conference (usually not a good idea) and announced a reduction of 275 positions, of which 119 were actual layoffs. The rest came from eliminating vacant positions. You would have thought that *every one* of the city's 4500 employees lost their jobs.

My intent was to deal with the issue quickly and decisively, but that proved to be the wrong path. Imagine the effect something like that might have on your organization. The reporters just couldn't wait. Who could blame them? This was news! They asked for the list of all the affected employees in order to interview them. Reporters got sound bites from those who were affected, while some council members wrung their hands saying how terrible it was, and it dominated the news for days. It didn't matter that other local governments in the region actually eliminated more jobs; what mattered was how I announced it—all in one day.

As a leader, you better learn from your mistakes pretty fast. As soon as the news hit, I turned to my staff and stated the obvious, "We're going to have some very hard years ahead and I mishandled this situation. We are not going to do it this way again. Let's regroup and figure out a better way." As for the bad press, all you can do is move forward and not be defensive. Not every decision you make or action you take will be correct.

In the years that followed, we had many more cutbacks. They were all made without fanfare. There's no need to get everyone in your organization upset when your cuts are carefully targeted. Each department made its own decision about reductions consistent with the organization's strategic goals, and made those reductions in a timely way. The cuts were made incrementally. We held no more press conferences about cuts and layoffs, and made no more big announcements. Most important, we had direct communication with the employees throughout the year so they understood our financial condition and how the decisions were being made.

I learned from that and every other mistake I made as mayor. Each time I erred I thought through where I had gone wrong and took the time to think clearly about how I could change my approach in the future. In every case, I did change my approach the next time around, even if it meant going against some ingrained habits. You have to fight the tendency to act defensively. Your growth as a leader is often reflected in how honest you are with yourself and acknowledging your shortcomings and learning from them.

In the workforce, if you want to be a real leader you must take responsibility not only for your own actions but for those of everyone on the organizational chart. As mayor, I made it clear to my staff that the ultimate responsibility was mine. Never would I point to an administrator or department head and say "He did it." The buck has to stop with someone and it's the person at the top. Interestingly, when your employees understand they are never going to be tossed to the wolves and you will take responsibility, they redouble their efforts to never make the mistake again. Setting that tone for your organization is important. It actually promotes a healthy self-evaluation among your team members so that *they* internalize the need to take responsibility. If their leader is a responsibility taker, they become responsibility takers too. You are helping to build leadership and accountability in your team.

We can recall the lack of responsibility that occurred during and after Hurricane Katrina. The mayor of New Orleans was busy blaming the state, the governor of Louisiana was busy blaming the federal government, and the president was congratulating the head of FEMA for a job well done although the country knew New Orleans was in trouble. No one stepped up to say, this is my responsibility, I am in charge and I am going to be responsible for fixing the problem.

Developing your inner leadership qualities means doing the unpleasant: confronting your mistakes, and taking full responsibility. There can be no finger-pointing and no excuses. Some fear that admitting a mistake means they won't get promoted. The reality is by not owning up to mistakes you won't ever become the leader who will achieve long-term success.

Compete Without Excuses

I have my physical education coach in elementary school to thank for an early lesson he instilled in me: compete without excuses. Physical education was much more rigorous in the 1960s than it is today. We had to run around the track to the hands of a stopwatch, climb ropes, and do a lot of things that today are probably prohibited. At the end of every week Coach Al Barnes would set up three concrete blocks and announce that week's winners. The fastest runners got to stand on the blocks and were honored. One day, I asked, "Coach Barnes, how come only boys get to stand on the blocks?"

"Because they run faster than the girls," he said.

Now I had a goal and for weeks I trained. I had my own stopwatch and every day after school I would sprint and test myself over and over again. Soon, there was a spot for me on one of those concrete blocks.

Coach Barnes made me a more competitive person, and to this day I appreciate that early lesson. He didn't create a fourth block for the fastest girl. He didn't give everybody a trophy to make them feel good. He simply told me what I had to accomplish. That's a good lesson. Competition starts with you. What is important is how fast *you* run, not how fast the other runners are.

Understanding competition and your role in the competitive process plays an important role in your ability to succeed. One day, my parents took me to listen to a woman who was running for election to the Hillsborough County Commission. Her name was Betty Castor, and she became the first woman elected to that position. The year was 1972 and I was 13. I didn't realize at the time that Betty was helping to usher in a new era in county government—a wave of progressive women who reshaped county government with a focus on the environment, growth management, and honesty. What I did see was retail politics. The candidate has to directly address an audience, answer questions, and ask for support. It wasn't about her opponent, it was about her performance. I can do that, I thought. I saw politics in a more personal light. It was doable—achievable. All I had to do was compete.

Years later, when I ran for the County Commission and in all my races thereafter, I was very competitive. After all, when you are in a race, you want to win. I have always seen competition for what it is—you up against any number of other qualified people. No special concrete block. Compete on your merits, win on your merits.

So often when people compete they are consumed with their opponent. I see this all the time in politics. Candidates talk incessantly about the strengths and weaknesses of the opposition. Campaign meetings drag on interminably while supporters swap stories about what the competition is up to.

I have never seen competition in that light because I compete against myself. I am my own critic and constantly push myself to do better. A campaign is about how I can win because I believe I am the best person for the job, not what the other candidates are doing. Getting on that concrete block in elementary school had nothing to do with how fast the other students ran, it had to do with how fast I ran. Compete with yourself and learn to compete without making excuses for yourself when you don't succeed.

An excellent example of someone who represents this straightforward leadership trait is Jeff Vinik, the owner of the National Hockey League's team, the Tampa Bay Lightning. Vinik is nationally known as a highly successful hedge fund manager who led the fabled Fidelity Magellan Fund in the 1990s. In 2010 he purchased the Tampa Bay Lightning, a team that had fallen considerably since its remarkable 2004 Stanley Cup Championship victory. After reaching that pinnacle, ownership changed hands several times and without clear direction and investment, the team languished. Vinik had a life-long love of the game. He purchased the team, developed a strategic plan for success, hired the best in the industry to recruit, manage, and coach, and led in a measured and thoughtful fashion. Though he and his wife and four children call Boston home, they established immediate ties to Tampa by buying a house and contributing $10 million to local charities. To enhance the Lightning fans' experience, he invested $40 million in upgrades to their arena. The team was reinvigorated by this display of straightforward leadership and played competitively in the 2011 Stanley Cup finals—a remarkable turnaround.

Vinik is a person who competes without excuses. He didn't arrive in Tampa to lay out a laundry list of why the team wasn't doing well and to expect others to fix the problems. He didn't blame the fans, the media, the arena, the government, corporate sales, or the weather. He didn't affix blame at all. Instead, he told a reporter:

My comments are genuine, my interest sincere. I will do everything in my power to bring a world-class organization to the community, both on the ice and off the ice. I am going to put the resources forth that are necessary to making this a successful organization.

A terrific example of competing without making excuses. The Lightning is a better team today because of Vinik's leadership qualities.

Build Resilience

I draw inspiration from our American history, which repeatedly reminds me how resilient we are as a people. The lessons I have learned from our country's past have sustained me through my years of leadership and enhanced my decision making. These lessons can help put anyone's life in perspective.

Our origins are compelling: the American Revolution, the writing and signing of the Declaration of Independence, the compromises that resulted in our Constitution, our first president, George Washington, and his judicious use of power. The great thinkers who created the intellectual basis for our country: Thomas Jefferson, John Adams, Benjamin Franklin, James Madison, and many more. These men were highly educated and possessed exceptional intellect. They were able to take what they knew of the world and create an ideal of something better. An experiment, yes, but one grounded in the idea that fundamentally people should be able to choose their own representatives and be a part of their government. As Lincoln later put it: "government of the people, by the people, for the people."

Before we could implement this new, radical idea of governance, we had to fight a war. The story of the American Revolution has to be the most implausible story in our entire history. Imagine, thirteen colonies, loosely woven together, declaring their independence from the world's superpower, Great Britain. The mere act of signing the Declaration of Independence was considered treason, and all who penned their names to it put their lives at risk. The royal court in London must have thought the colonists were out of their minds to take them on. England had a vast army and navy and plenty of money with which to wage war. The colonists? They had an army of sorts called the Continental Army led by General George Washington. The army was poorly clothed, ill-equipped, and poorly fed. There was no navy. Money? Sometimes it was appropriated and sometimes not. The Continental Army is often referred to in history books as ragtag and it seems an apt description.

As Americans we love to celebrate the year 1776 because it marks the signing of the Declaration of Independence. Let us not forget, however, that 1776 almost marked the end of our revolutionary experiment. Our Continental Army got off to a very poor start. If they had had cable news back then, the pundits would have been calling for Washington's resignation. (For a compelling read on this pivotal year, I recommend David McCullough's, 1776.)[2]

In 1776, Washington suffered one defeat after another. In a span of three months, he lost the battles of Brooklyn, Kips Bay, White Plains and Fort Washington. When his diminished army reached Newark in late November, the troops were in such sorry shape it inspired Thomas Paine to write, "These are the times that try men's souls."

The British General Cornwallis was confident that he could put an end to the revolutionary uprising. With an army of 10,000 men he set out to trap Washington in New Jersey. Washington kept moving, arriving on the Pennsylvania side of the Delaware River on December 2, 1776. It was bitterly cold and his remaining men had inadequate clothing and food. The state of the revolution at this point was precarious. Congress had fled Philadelphia. Local citizens were signing on with the British, afraid the uprising would end and they would be accused of treason. All seemed hopeless.

---

2. David McCullough, 1776, New York: Simon & Schuster, 2005.

Washington had a plan. His army would re-cross the Delaware River on Christmas day, surprising the Hessian soldiers, German mercenaries paid by England to fight, who occupied Trenton. The element of surprise was critical to his success. Washington crossed the Delaware on Christmas night. As if their luck could get any worse, an ice storm hit as they were crossing. It was perilous. They arrived in Trenton in the early morning of December 26. The attack on Trenton began, and in under an hour the Americans had captured the city. The Hessians had been out drinking a bit too much the night before, celebrating Christmas. They picked the wrong day to sleep in.

Fortified by the supplies of food and clothing in Trenton, and the sense of renewed confidence their victory gave them, the Continental Army went on to win another victory at Princeton on January 3, 1777. These battles turned the fortunes of the Revolution and gave the Continental Army the spirit with which to fight another day.

And fight they did. The war lasted another six and half years, finally ending in 1783. Twenty-five thousand Americans lost their lives. In the end, this small band of revolutionaries defeated the greatest superpower then on earth. An unbelievable story even hundreds of years later. The revolutionary war lasted nearly eight years; it was certainly no overnight success. Our long and painful trudge towards freedom demonstrated our determination and resiliency. These traits have defined us ever since.

I have seen many examples of strength and resiliency. These are qualities that are crucial to straightforward leadership. So many stories have inspired me over the years. In August 2009, one of our police officers, Andrea Law, was in a serious car accident while she was vacationing in Mexico with friends. She was airlifted to Tampa where her condition was critical. Her liver had been sliced in half and she suffered an injury to her brain.

I hadn't personally known Andrea prior to the accident though I pinned a badge on her when she was sworn in as a police officer.

Known to her friends and family as "Dre," she had, as I soon discovered, a larger-than-life personality and more friends than anyone I know. The waiting room outside of the intensive care unit became the "Dre's Friends Club" with a 24-hour-a-day vigil. Her parents flew in from Ohio and were immediately enveloped by this wide circle of friends. Police Chief Jane Castor and I were at the hospital every day to see how Andrea was progressing. The prognosis was grim. I soon bonded with her mother, Cheryl, who was strong and spiritual. We shared many moments together, just mom to mom.

The doctors amazingly put Andrea's liver back together. The brain injury still loomed. She was on a ventilator and the doctors were gloomy about her chances for recovery. I was with Cheryl when the doctors told her there really was no hope for her daughter. She wouldn't live. The injury was too severe. If she did live she wouldn't be able to care for herself. Cheryl looked at me and said, "I know my daughter and she is trying to live. She will make it. I will not give up on her." I felt at that moment as if a strong gust of wind had swept through the hospital corridor. I felt hope.

Andrea's parents took Dre back to Ohio where she went into rehabilitation. Her progress was remarkable. In November 2010, Cheryl, Dre, a few of her many friends, and I had lunch together in Tampa. When Dre walked through the door of the restaurant, I cried. She could walk, talk, eat, and laugh. She has come back to her home at the Tampa Police Department. Dre and her mother are inspirations. Dre's story is one illustration of inner strength that many people don't know they possess until adversity hits.

Perhaps the most striking example of this resiliency was the appearance of Congresswoman Gabrielle Giffords on the floor of the House of Representatives in August 2011 as the House cast a pivotal vote to raise the nation's debt ceiling. Just eight months after being shot in the head by an assailant, she made the trip and cast a vote that she believed was important to our country. Her recovery and her resolve are a testament to her straightforward leadership style.

Sometimes people can't see this trait in themselves. So often I have heard employees or friends say, "I can't" when in fact they can. Part of developing your inner leadership qualities is recognizing your own strengths and realizing you can accomplish more than you think you can. Over and over as mayor I saw examples of citizens tentatively approaching city government in order to get an issue resolved. After a while they grew comfortable in their newfound leadership roles and soon became regular fixtures at city council meetings. Through participation in the civic process they began to develop their inner leadership qualities.

Our country has weathered many difficult times yet we always emerge stronger. It is no different in your personal or professional life. You will be tested and may occasionally fail. You will face obstacles. Some challenges may seem insurmountable. I encourage you to dig deep and find that inner strength. Tap into your resiliency and see yourself as a person capable of leading.

Show Respect for Others

As I have grown older and have had the benefit of running a large organization, I have learned to appreciate the importance of showing respect to everyone. It may not be taught in business school, but kindness and respect are fundamental to success. If success is about relationships, then acts of kindness are the glue that binds those relationships.

When I was growing up in the 1960s and 1970s, most of the bosses on sitcom television shows tended to be grumpy. They hauled people into their offices and hollered at them. It made for funny TV but it's not so funny in real life.

As a young elected county commissioner I had plenty to learn. Given my youth and inexperience I looked for ways to improve. I hadn't acquired too many bad habits because I had scant experience in the workforce. I wanted to do well in my new capacity and I learned from two early mistakes.

When first elected to the county commission, I was sometimes too sharp with the county staff during public meetings. My questions were pointed and if the answers didn't flow the way I thought they should, I became impatient and it showed. Looking back, I suspect I was immature. It was not appropriate behavior. There was no single turning point, but I quickly decided that acting in an authoritarian, stern manner at the dais was not the right style for me. It ended.

Right from the start I also learned a lesson about being respectful when you are in a position of power. If you go to local legislative meetings at which the public has been invited to speak, you'll see many of the elected officials talking to one another instead of listening to the speakers. These sidebar conversations are epidemic in our society and occur in staff meetings, speeches, and most forums where there is a speaker. Apparently, the thought of simply listening to a speaker for a certain length of time is too much to bear. It was one of my first county commission meetings. As members of the public spoke, a fellow commissioner leaned over to talk to me. I responded and we had a laugh over something.

Afterwards, an older woman came up to me; she was not happy. "I voted for you and I think you have potential. You are rude to talk while the public is speaking. It's time and money to come downtown to speak our mind. And while I'm speaking, you are talking to someone else! I'm really disappointed in you."

And I thought, "She's absolutely right."

I never did it again. Over the years, if someone leaned over to talk to me during public comment, I would politely push away. This early lesson has helped me immeasurably. I wish everyone in a position of power had the benefit of that woman's counsel, which has held me accountable to a higher, more respectful level of decorum.

When I was in college at The American University in Washington, D.C., my roommate's parents took us to dinner at a fancy Washington restaurant. At the next table was Joseph Califano, who at that time was in President Jimmy Carter's Cabinet. Imagine our excitement—two political science undergraduates with a Cabinet secretary at the next table! At some point we went over to his table to say hello. What a spectacle we must have made of ourselves; it was an inappropriate thing to do. I remember saying, "I'm just a student." His response was very gracious. "Being a student of government is very important," he said, and then proceeded to ask us questions about our studies. He even shared a little bit about what he was working on at the time. We interrupted his dinner, but he was completely kind and welcoming. I never forgot it.

I will also never forget the lack of kindness of the congressman for whom I interned on Capitol Hill. Fortunately, I didn't have much interaction with him, but from what I observed he made most of the staff miserable. He was a yeller and an unhappy sort. I vowed that if I ever became an elected official, I would be nothing like him. After I graduated from college, I was offered a real job in his office. I declined. The reason? I thought the congressman was unkind.

> "Kindness reflects a basic respect for people."

I know we all have our failings and there have been plenty of times that I haven't been as nice as I should have been. Being irritable because of lack of sleep or stress is just an excuse. I always feel better about myself when I'm nice to everyone—even my political opponents. There is no satisfaction to be gained from being unpleasant. The old image of the grumpy boss is outdated. Today, respectful and kind behavior wins out.

Kindness reflects a basic respect for people—a respect for others even when you are under pressure, or don't feel well, or don't particularly like the person you're with. It's about the other person feeling good about being in your presence. It is an underpinning of effective leadership and the habit of exhibiting kindness and respect leads to a richer life.

Exercise Power Carefully

As he so often did, President Lincoln said it all: "Nearly all men can stand adversity, but if you want to test a man's character, give him power."

Power — especially the desire for power — is an interesting topic. Some people don't care if they have much power, but some people crave it. At its best, power can produce good results. At its worst, it is abusive.

In the city of Tampa, the mayor is the CEO of the city, which has a "strong mayor" form of government. The mayor has complete authority over the executive branch and veto power over acts of the city council. The position wields a lot of power. The greater the power you are given, the more careful you need to be in how you use it.

I was often amazed by how many people would say to me, "Pam, you're the mayor. Call so-and-so into your office and read him the riot act. You tell him the way it's going to be." In their view, that was an appropriate use of power.

Operating in that way would be neither effective nor desirable. The role of mayor is that of the chief convener of the community, the chief collaborator. The position requires bringing people together to find common ground and solutions to our shared problems. Every person deserves courtesy and a hearing. Wielding a heavy hand with people in the community or on city council is inappropriate and ultimately counterproductive.

Imagine the tone set for the community if people were harangued when they visited the mayor's office. Picture staff members living in fear of being called in to be admonished. The climate you set as a leader is one of the most important elements of your job. An atmosphere of fear and abusive behavior diminishes you and the position you hold.

Any observer of politics sees the corrupting influence of power. You give someone a title, a leather chair, an aide or two, and put them on a dais where they look down on other people, but unless they are centered and understand the "servant" part of "public servant," things go awry. Power can corrupt. I've seen it happen so many times, even when the amount of power is tiny and the position relatively minor.

Consider what happens when an insecure person is elected to public office. Suddenly, they are fawned over by lobbyists and staff and told that they are special. The official starts believing what others are saying, and sometimes begins to act badly.

I believe people who abuse power have low self-esteem. Every time I meet a pompous, arrogant individual, I see someone who doesn't feel good about himself. Something has happened in his journey through life and he's built this persona to make up for deficiencies. They are using their position and power as a substitute for what they lack in their personal lives.

Before you promote someone to a position of authority within your organization, look at the totality of the person. Is he secure, happy, and willing to acknowledge shortcomings? Is he humble, introspective, and centered? People who are comfortable in their own skin are nice to everyone.

A major problem in our country today is excessive partisanship, which is a distortion of power. Because it is viewed as the power of the party and not as individual power, it is easier to be abusive. If you are part of a legislative body and don't vote your party line, you can be stripped of your committee chairmanship or your office may be moved to the basement. This is an abuse of power, but, because it is done under the cloak of "party politics," it is accepted as a way of doing business. The reality is no matter how you frame it, when you have authority over someone else, be it in business, politics, or your personal life, you should exercise care, caution, and kindness.

Politics is an incredible example of how power affects leaders in good and bad ways. But it is really no different in the corporate world, just less visible to the public. As mayor, I visited dozens of corporate offices, factories, and warehouses to gain a better understanding of a company's product or service. Always I came away with more information than how a product was physically made. I was able to see how the CEO wielded power. Companies that thrived had CEOs who cared about their employees and treated them as they would want to be treated. They knew about the family of the man working in the warehouse, they easily conversed and joked with all employees. Their employees were a team, looking out for one another and supporting the overall mission of the organization. Successful CEOs saw their role as a bridge between the overall big picture mission of the organization and the welfare of the people employed to carry out the mission. There was a caring, sincere connection that was healthy and meaningful. The power these CEOs exerted was always used to build others up, and, in doing so to elevate the entire company. It was not used to puff themselves up or knock someone else down.

How you use power says a lot about you. Developing your inner leadership qualities involves getting a firm grip on how you will exercise power throughout your life. Once your style is developed it can be hard to change. It is important to make a conscious, deliberative decision about how you are going to use whatever power you have and to be consistent in your application of it.

The Path to Straightforward Leadership: Step 1—Inner Leadership

In this chapter we examined the inner leadership qualities you need to be a straightforward leader and we identified the important traits common to exemplary leaders:

- The necessity for honest self-evaluation to see where improvement is needed, and
- The importance of embarking on a continual path of growth and change so that these characteristics become firmly embedded in your leadership style

A clear-eyed view of your strengths and weaknesses and a desire to become better are essential. Straightforward leadership is not for the person who can't be introspective, or the one who doesn't see the need for self-improvement. It takes a person eager to work hard, willing to make a conscious, consistent effort to develop inner leadership qualities, and with genuine humility to see himself as a work in progress. The challenge, if you want to improve as a leader, is to see the inevitable failings and to vow to change for the better.

In the next four chapters, we will discuss how these traits are applied to the process of leading.

Chapter Two

—◦◦◦—

BECOME A PERSON OF SUBSTANCE

INNER LEADERSHIP QUALITIES MAKE THE leader. One way to measure a straightforward leader is by the proficiencies, skills and initiatives that integrate leadership qualities with their day to day practical application. A key competency is substance, by which I mean what a person actually does, knows and how he ethically leads—not what he says—and it is an essential part of becoming a true leader.

My friend and advisor Fred Karl once lamented to me about a top administrator: "The problem, when it's all said and done, is there's a lot more said than done." That in a nutshell is the problem of working with an employee without substance! Anyone who has ever worked has encountered this type of person. Some get by and contribute in small ways to an organization. Some even manage to get promoted despite their lack of gravitas. In fact, the person Fred spoke of was later recruited and promoted by another entity.

The ability to get promoted should not be confused with leadership ability. A real leader—a straightforward leader—is one who can get the job done. To become that kind of leader, you must strengthen your core traits and exhibit the proficiencies and skills needed to excel.

You know you have achieved substance when:

- *You are an authority on the subject*: No one wants to be led by someone who doesn't have a firm understanding of their subject matter, can't deal with facts in a credible manner, and doesn't have the ability to convey the organization's mission.
- *You communicate with a confidence, which is reflected in your tone, message and the image you convey*: It is not enough for a straightforward leader to be knowledgeable; the ability to communicate is an absolute must and central to inspiring the organization.
- *You choose wise, trusted, and honest mentors*: A confidant who gives you honest criticism and guidance helps you grow.
- *You hire people who know more than you do*: Have the confidence to assemble the very best staff that can make the organization successful.
- *You make learning a lifetime priority*: Never stop acquiring new information and applying this knowledge to the team.

Become an Authority, Build Credibility

I had the pleasure of getting to know General David Petraeus while I was mayor and he was the head of the U.S. Central Command (CENTCOM) stationed in Tampa. We socialized several times and he and his wife Holly came to our home for dinner. General Petraeus has all of the attributes of a straightforward leader, but what struck me most when we spoke was his mastery of history, the Middle East, and his broad understanding of global issues. He is a multidimensional public figure who combines intellect with practical sensibilities. It did not surprise me that President Obama turned to General Petraeus to run the war in Afghanistan and later the Central Intelligence Agency. He is a leader of real substance.

This is immediately apparent from his background. From his graduation as a "distinguished cadet" at West Point, to winning the top graduate award from the U.S. Army Command and General Staff College Class, to earning a PhD degree in international relations from Princeton University's Woodrow Wilson School of Public and International Affairs, General Petraeus demonstrated his desire to accumulate knowledge and become an expert in his field. He served in numerous challenging capacities across the world and shined at each. No wonder Congress members on both sides of the aisle pay attention when he testifies; he is an authority and he has the credibility.

In politics I have always respected former Florida governor and senator, Bob Graham, as an example of a straightforward leader who built his credibility on the accumulation of knowledge. Graham is known for writing down details of his daily activities in small notebooks that he always carries with him. These notebooks, filled with facts and observations, convey a curious mind. Graham is interested in people and issues and it shows. While serving in the United States Senate, Graham chaired the Senate Select Committee on Intelligence and became an expert on intelligence matters. After 9/11, he co-chaired a joint inquiry into the attack. In 2004 he wrote a book that revealed serious deficiencies in our national security system. As a result of his in-depth knowledge, he is a national resource on the subject and can always be counted upon to give a thoughtful and analytical response to a question. Unlike so many of our politicians who speak in sound bites and talking points supplied by their political party, Graham gives comprehensive answers to questions because he is a person of substance.

Though he has been out of public office for years, he is still called upon to assist our nation when it is in need of trustworthy and fair direction in complicated situations. He served on the Financial Crisis Inquiry Commission after the financial meltdown in 2008 and co-chaired the BP Deepwater Horizon Oil Spill and Offshore Drilling Commission. People know him to be a man of integrity — both measured and thoughtful. This is the hallmark of the straightforward leader, an individual who has earned widespread respect not only for his knowledge but his ability to tackle problems head-on and tell the unvarnished truth.

Being an authority in your field and building credibility are linked to many of the inner leadership qualities, including the ability to be honest and humble, measured and thoughtful, and to freely admit mistakes, and accept responsibility. Every organization needs an honest and credible leader that establishes ethical standards and then reinforces them. The more you demonstrate credibility, the more you earn, and the more it grows. Credibility ought to be established *before* a crisis erupts. When something bad happens — an environmental mishap, an inconclusive election, an employee scandal — your reputation and that of your organization needs to be firmly established so you can weather the crisis. It can't be artificially created by public relations specialists after the fact.

Becoming an authority and building your credibility doesn't happen overnight. Time brings wisdom and each experience adds value as you grow into a leadership role. The days of the generalist are over, so it is even more important to develop a body of knowledge. Look at the résumés and accomplishments of those you admire and you will see substantive leaders whose continuous growth and upward mobility is linked to their growing expertise.

Develop Effective Communication Skills

Remember Texas billionaire Ross Perot and his 1992 independent bid for the presidency? He purchased 30-minute blocks of airtime to present his views primarily on the growing budget deficit and debt. Armed with pie charts and bar graphs, he explained how running in the red affects every American. His message was easy to understand; he took a complex issue and reduced it to a simple chart. His clarity was likely responsible for the fact that he garnered 19 percent of the popular vote in the 1992 general election, a real feat for a third party candidate.

Simple but effective communication is an important part of a substantive leader's skill set. We could use a few pie charts today to help Americans better understand our debt issues. Having the best idea, the best product, or the best service is great, but if you can't articulate these assets, how can you be successful?

I entered elective politics in the 1980s and soon understood that my effectiveness came down to my ability to persuade three other county commissioners to see my point of view. Talking and making motions wasn't going to produce results if I couldn't get others to second my motions. What to do? I learned that to be effective, I first had to listen and understand what motivated my fellow commissioners. Then, I had to figure out where we had common ground. With almost everyone, you probably hold some shared view. Finding that commonality and building on it leads to real partnerships.

As I became accustomed to almost daily presentations from staff members, constituents and consultants, I concluded that simple and short was better. To me, the mark of a valuable employee or consultant is the ability to describe both the problem and the proposed solution in about fifteen minutes.

I'll never forget attending a special workshop on wastewater sludge management. The lights dimmed and on came a consultant with a slide presentation. These were pre-PowerPoint days. In short order, most of the commissioners were asleep. I bent over to one of my still-awake colleagues and asked, "Is this a legitimate quorum if the majority is asleep?"

39

Every year, during my tenure as mayor, we asked department directors to summarize for the other senior staff what their achievable goals were for the coming year. In order to hear from all the department heads before the year was up, we limited each to their top three goals and a presentation no longer than five minutes. Even with those ground rules, most just couldn't do it. Some went beyond three goals, some went way beyond five minutes, and some just couldn't sum it all up.

"The fewer words you use, the more valuable they are."

Granted, this was an opportunity for the directors to demonstrate their areas of expertise. After all, the mayor was there, and how many opportunities do you get to really showcase your work? The more face time the better. Right?

For me, the opposite is true. The less said the better. People of substance find ways to make their point succinctly. Everyone will appreciate you more.

I learned the importance of communication skills when I was the Supervisor of Elections and trained nearly 4,000 poll workers. The poll workers run each precinct, greet each voter, and make sure the election is run correctly. Initially, we hired professional trainers to perform this important task. After the first election in which I served as supervisor, it became clear that the key to successful elections was well-trained poll workers, and that I needed to show them that I understood their challenges. Once I became a true authority on the election process and understood what the poll workers faced, I conducted the training classes myself.

My involvement in our training did more to produce smooth elections than anything we could have put in place. Teaching the poll workers directly helped us build a rapport, and on Election Day they knew how important it was to get certain procedures absolutely right. Each poll worker received the same information in the same manner, so all voters were treated equally in all precincts. Further, you build loyalty when the people working in the field see the person in charge immersed in the details of their work. There is no substitute for understanding your employees' problems and challenges.

After the 2000 presidential election debacle, in 2002 we moved from punch card technology to touch screen technology. The importance of strong and consistent training was further heightened. The machines were more complex and the procedures more technical than the punch cards had been. So much was at stake in this transition. I had been an advocate for election reform, including the move to touch screen, and didn't want a poorly run election after the investment in improved technology. One night, I sat straight up in bed thinking—"Three points! That's it!"

The next morning I wrote down the three most important details I wanted the poll workers to remember. These were the top three items that, no matter what else happened on Election Day, had to get done. My staff put them in large letters on colored paper. During training sessions, I went through the entire poll worker manual and we practiced using the machines. At the end of the class, I handed each of them the colored sheet.

"You can make any mistake on Election Day except these three. Place this under your pillow at night and make sure you do these three things correctly," I instructed. Of course, they all had a good laugh and thought it was funny that I had distilled the entire election down to something so simple. "Simple is beautiful." You can guess the outcome. Not a single poll worker made an error on any of these three things. When I visited precincts on Election Day, poll workers would proudly hold up the colored sheet and inform me they had done all three correctly.

The lesson: we often communicate too much information. Most people can absorb only a certain amount of material. Even when I hear a really good speaker and listen intently to every word, I can usually remember only two or three points when I recount the experience. Think through what you are trying to communicate and be sensitive to the fact that your audience can't possibly absorb it all. A leader of substance has to find ways to make key points memorable.

Success in running a city is largely about communicating effectively. Not only do you have to transmit your strategic goals and ideas to your staff, heads of various departments, and council members, but you also have to communicate them to the community, which means getting your message across to people with all different levels of understanding. One day you might be talking to a small group of neighborhood leaders who want to make sure their issues are heard and resolved. The next day it is a group of businesspeople interested in global trade opportunities. By the end of the week, you may have made a dozen or more speeches or presentations and held smaller meetings with numerous groups. All of this adds up to the overall impression the community forms of your organization and leadership.

Your communication has to be consistent and continuous. It should be two-way; listening often is as effective as speaking. The thirtieth president of the United States, Calvin Coolidge, was known as a man of few words. "No man ever listened his way out of a job," Coolidge remarked. Indeed, what Coolidge apparently lacked in conversational skills, he made up for in listening. Both are important parts of the communication process.

There's nothing quite like a bad experience to teach you how to better communicate. As described earlier, in 2007 I mishandled the way I communicated layoffs and budget cuts. As a result, I got nothing but bad press and a worried workforce. After evaluating what I had done wrong, I concluded the city's employees needed direct and clear information about our ongoing financial situation. I embarked on becoming the educator-in-chief, explaining our budget issues directly to employees several hundred at a time.

Looking back, I wonder why I didn't communicate directly with our employees from the beginning of my term. There was no substitute for my direct understanding of how they viewed their work environment and the financial cutbacks.

Even with direct communication, if the message is not repeated continually, it's hard to make it stick. In my fourth and final year of the annual meetings, which I started in my second term, I asked city employees how many city workers they believed had lost their jobs due to the cutbacks. The facts were that after cutting $124 million from the budget, we had eliminated 672 positions. 235 workers lost their jobs, and the rest of the positions were vacant. This was in the context of a workforce of approximately 4500. I showed them pie charts that explained the breakdown. They were astonished. Based on hearsay, they believed that nearly a thousand employees had lost their jobs. While they had heard the facts from me at each annual meeting, the message had not been repeated often enough.

> "Communication is the immune system of an organization."

Nonetheless, direct communication with our employees made a huge difference. Although not everyone was won over, as the years passed city workers were more relaxed and had a greater understanding of what we were up against.

Communicate in a way everyone can understand. The first year, I tried to explain what the Florida Legislature had enacted that caused our budget to shrink. That didn't work. Many people didn't keep up with state politics and couldn't make the connection between laws passed by the Florida Legislature and their own personal job situation. When the Great Recession hit, I initially compared it to the Great Depression of the 1930s. I wasn't getting much of a response, judging from the eye contact and body language. I realized that comparing something to a long-ago historical event isn't meaningful to everyone. My analogy doesn't work if the employee is not familiar with the Great Depression. It just didn't resonate. So I got down to basics.

"Do you think your home is worth more today than last year?"

"Do you have a neighbor or a friend who lost their job?"

That they could relate to.

My final year in office I decided to negotiate directly with the three labor unions. I promised each three meetings, but no more. If we couldn't iron out our differences, we would go back to the usual method of staff negotiations—a drawn-out process that nobody liked. Each contract was hammered out in three meetings. Frank communication—it worked for me.

Salesmanship is all about effective communication. In politics, you start by selling yourself. The campaign is one giant sales promotion. If successful, you are given a chance to serve. Once elected, the sales focus shifts from the campaign to the strategic goals and the ideas of the administration. Effecting major change takes constant and effective communication.

As the chief salesperson for the city, it was my job to sell its merits to outsiders as well as to excite the residents about the virtues of their hometown. Being the city's principal booster was easy because I love our city and truly believe in its greatness. That's the first key to any good salesperson—sincere passion.

People like enthusiasm. How many times have you bought something and been impressed by the knowledge and excitement the salesperson had for the product? Whether it's a car, an appliance, or a financial product, I love it when the salesperson truly believes in what they're selling. If you are in sales, you have to believe in your product and establish a sense that the customer will be better off for having bought it.

Two major sales presentations I was involved in were unforgettable and illustrate the importance of passion that is derived from your expertise. In 2005, we were bidding for Super Bowl XLIII. Tampa had successfully hosted three previous Super Bowls. This time we were up against stiff competition: Atlanta, Miami, and Houston. The scuttlebutt was that Atlanta had it in the bag because they had just made major improvements to their stadium.

Undeterred, our group dutifully flew to Washington, D.C. to make our presentation. Everywhere we went, the word was Atlanta.

Yet we kept our spirits high. We knew the other cities were making good presentations, but we truly believed that we had the best product. Our civic pride was unmatched.

In the presentation room were all of the NFL team owners. The Glazer family, owners of the Tampa Bay Buccaneers, went all out on our community's behalf talking to the other owners. When we made our presentation, our collective passion came through and we all felt that we had hit it out of the ballpark. When the text message came through announcing the selection—Tampa—it was truly emotional.

Our entire team demonstrated straightforward leadership during that presentation. We stayed positive, were respectful of the competition, and were resilient in the face of seemingly insurmountable odds. We were a substantive group, all experts not only in our community and its capacity to host the event, but also knowledgeable about the NFL and what the owners' expectations were. Our communication was effective as well as honest, direct, and enthusiastic.

Also important: when we did host that Super Bowl in February 2009 we lived up to all of our promises. If we told the NFL we were going to do something, we did it. That's the most important part of sales—fulfilling the promise and maintaining our future credibility.

The second major presentation occurred in 2009 when we bid for the 2012 Republican National Convention. Tampa had been in contention before, but had not been successful. The State of Florida had not hosted a political convention since 1972. We felt strongly that the time was right for Tampa and the state to host such a premier event.

Talk about civic pride! We had every part of our community highlighted and went all out to show the RNC delegation everything we could offer. The final sales push was at a dinner in Ybor City, our historic district. Similar to the Super Bowl effort, we poured our passion into our presentations. It came as no surprise to me when it was announced that Tampa would host the 2012 Republican National Convention. I knew we had given it our very best.

Having an emotional tie to what you are selling makes it easy to promote. If you are in sales, you may not be as emotional about your product as I am about the City of Tampa, but to be successful you have to have a level of pride and passion about what you do. A sale is about getting others to believe as you do, but first you have to believe. You have to be substantive in your field to have this passion.

Not every sales effort will be successful. I was part of a large-scale effort to sell a sales tax increase to the public to pay for mass transit improvements that did not pass a voter referendum largely because we violated the simplicity rule of communication. I learned many lessons from the experience.

It is easy to communicate simple messages. "As mayor I want to encourage residential housing in our downtown." Or, "We are building the Tampa Riverwalk to open up the river to the people." Those messages are easy to understand and discuss with voters.

Transportation issues are not so easy to communicate, particularly when some of the issues are of a technical nature. In Hillsborough County, a plan was developed to build light rail, a better bus system that included various types of buses, and roads. It was presented as one large package with a large price tag requiring funding in perpetuity.

I have long advocated for mass transit in our community. While Tampa has many assets, it lacks a modern transit system and we need to take the next step to light rail and a better, more modern bus system. Tampa is the only metropolitan area of its size except Detroit that does not have a modern rail system. Starting in 2006, I wove the mass transit theme into my speeches. I was speaking theoretically because no specific plan had yet been adopted by the transit company or the county commission. I could tell that audiences wanted the transit; in fact, they were ahead of their public officials in their thinking. After every speech people would ask, "When can we vote on this? We need it!"

As the years passed, the county moved towards producing a plan. With so many people involved and different constituencies with varied needs, the plan grew in an attempt to accommodate what everyone wanted. The result was a big plan that was almost impossible to explain. The referendum was set for November 2010.

While the early support was promising, as we drew closer to the referendum, support waned. The first problem was the economy. The Great Recession had taken root, with high unemployment and property values plummeting from their peak in 2006. You couldn't have asked for a worse time to place a sales tax referendum on the ballot.

Even the impact of the bad economy could have been overcome if the plan had been simpler. My instincts told me failure was inevitable because it took too long to explain the package. It took at least twenty minutes to lay out the basic facts, explain light rail, different forms of bus service, and the complex financing. After fielding questions, I sensed that the majority of the audience was for the referendum, but only because they heard the detailed explanation. After one presentation a man came up to me and said, "Mayor, if everyone could hear the presentation you just gave with all of the details, it would pass." My heart sank. While I could convince an audience of 50 people, we needed to convince hundreds of thousands of voters, and most voters weren't going to hear all the details. It just wasn't possible to effectively communicate the merits of the issue to such a large audience.

In spite of the defeat, the effort was worthwhile and laid the groundwork for future funding for mass transit improvements in our community and region. While we haven't yet drawn victory from the jaws of defeat, those of us who fought for it see it as the first step toward producing a plan that one day will be adopted.

The referendum taught me a big lesson about communicating. You have to start with a product or issue that can be easily explained.

In hindsight, it would have been easier to sell one light rail line paid for with a sales tax that would expire in 20 years. If successful, it could have demonstrated to the public how this new form of transportation could benefit them. Small measurable steps that are easily understood and where success is demonstrable are the most effective. If you can't easily explain your cause, your product, or your idea in a single paragraph, you are going to have a tough time gaining support. This was a hard lesson, but you learn through trial and error. In sales you lose more often than you win. But the losses can be valuable as long as you learn something from them and apply them to the next prospect.

A substantive leader develops a communication style that is simple, direct, and credible. Read your audience at all times and evaluate how they are reacting to the quality of the information and the delivery. Whether you are transmitting information to employees, the public, shareholders, customers, or the media, remember to think simplicity and clarity.

Find Positive Mentors

Behind every successful person, there usually is a positive mentor. A good strong mentor who truly cares about you can help you prevent catastrophic mistakes that can ruin a career. A mentor can help you develop your inner leadership qualities and an understanding of the importance of continual growth and change.

There are examples of mentor relationships aplenty in our history but one that deserves a look is the relationship between a young Teddy Roosevelt and a wilderness guide from Island Falls, Maine named Bill Sewall. When Roosevelt arrived in Maine he was a sickly youngster who had just lost his father. Sewall helped Roosevelt face his health challenges head on. With his mentor as his guide, Roosevelt not only developed an appreciation for the rugged outdoors, but most importantly, he developed an inner strength that helped him conquer his physical weakness and build a robust character.[3] The memorable president and leader Theodore Roosevelt we know from the history books had Sewall to thank for much of his development.

When you emulate the inner strengths and positive traits of a successful person you admire and can relate to, you evolve into a leader of greater substance. Many people count their parents as mentors, and some view people they have never met but admire from a distance as mentors and role models. Whoever your mentor is, he or she can help you grow. If you have a personal relationship with your mentor, a strong level of trust on your part and a genuine concern and caring about your future on your mentor's part has to exist. The most impactful mentoring occurs when the person is not just a wise, guiding force, but a close personal friend, who can guide you with the emotional attachment of a real friendship. Honest feedback from someone who truly cares about both your personal and professional life is an enriching relationship that shapes you as a person.

I have been fortunate to have that kind of mentor and friend in my life, a person who has been a constant guide since I was 22, and who has offered counsel through the best and worst of times.

Back home in Tampa after graduating from The American University in Washington D.C., I hosted a cable television talk show for a small cable station in Temple Terrace. Back then, cable TV was just starting, and this show fulfilled a public affairs programming requirement.

Called "Community Focus," the half-hour program spotlighted local politics. Although I knew that the show had few viewers, the elected officials I called didn't—and I didn't tell them—so they all agreed to appear. One by one, I met city council members, county commissioners, and candidates running for office. At the time, Fran

"Be open to new people, one of them just might be your mentor-in-waiting."

---

3. Andrew Vietze, *Becoming Teddy Roosevelt: How a Maine Guide Inspired America's 26th President*, Camden, ME: Down East Books, 2010.

Davin was a highly respected, two-term county commissioner in Hillsborough County. She came on the show and we had a good interview. Fran is an engaging person and she's interested in other people. We walked out to the car together and spent a long time talking. Fran likes to talk but she's also the best listener I've ever known. The next year, when she ran for an open seat in the Florida House, she asked me to be her campaign coordinator. During that campaign, I saw in Fran the kind of public official I wanted to be.

That little cable show led to a friendship that has lasted for three decades. Wise, intelligent, and generous in spirit, she was clearly someone I could look up to and learn from. Perhaps our common love of politics drew us to one another. Fran provided the strategy for my first race for the county commission and has been the driving force behind every campaign since. Beyond the campaigns, she has shown me how to be a better person and a better public official. I would not have been successful in my political life without Fran. She helped me develop a straightforward leadership style and she always reminds me of the need to continually work on developing inner leadership qualities.

The key value of a mentor is having someone who will always be honest with you. We frequently are not honest with ourselves. A mentor can help us keep it real and prompt the all-important introspection leaders require. Every CEO, indeed any person in a top leadership position, needs someone in their life who will be straight with them—someone unfazed by a title or success, someone who tells you when you are approaching a problem the wrong way. A mentor broadens you and helps you reflect on yourself. An essential part of being a substantive leader is the ability to grow and learn from good, honest, sound advice.

Hire Smart People and Give Them Credit

From the outside the organization seemed fine. It was widely respected and its CEO often lauded. However, disagreements with the Board of

Directors caused the CEO to step down and in the interim the number two person was put in charge. The result over the next several months was chaos. The number two was completely ineffectual. Other staff jockeyed for position as rumors and backstabbing ran rampant.

I wish I could say this case is unusual but, unfortunately, it is not. As mayor, I witnessed it many times in business, government, and non-profits. The result always reinforced my belief that straight-forward leaders surround themselves with people whose skill sets exceed their own. Weakness below signals weakness at the top.

Effective leadership means knowing yourself, your strengths and your weaknesses. It's essential when performing one of a leader's most important tasks—hiring your team. I can tell very quickly if a leader is secure and has the attributes of an authentic leader by the staff they hire and their succession planning. Beware the leader whose team lacks someone of quality who could step into the number one position. The lack of a strong number two usually indicates that number one is insecure and doesn't want someone in his organization who could pose a threat.

A poor leader doesn't want people of greater talent than theirs on the team. Instead they hire people who profess loyalty to them—not necessarily to the organization. This is the "entourage" CEO, the person who likes to have staff around him at all times. The staff's personal loyalty is what matters to such leaders. Their weakness makes him seem more able by contrast and conveys a greater stature than he deserves. The leader's inability to surround himself with top quality people means he is uncomfortable having his mental or technical skills challenged.

President Abraham Lincoln is one of the best examples of a self-assured leader who surrounded himself with individuals who possessed far greater experience than he. Remember, when Lincoln assumed the presidency he had scant experience in the national arena having only served a single term in Congress. His string of electoral defeats was legendary.

As detailed in the fascinating book, *Team of Rivals*,[4] by historian Doris Kearns Goodwin, Lincoln not only appointed men with more experience than he had, he even appointed William H. Seward, Salmon P. Chase, and Edward Bates—all men of distinguished backgrounds who had been his rivals for the Republican nomination. In fact, many journalists at the time of Lincoln's inauguration considered Seward, who was Secretary of State, a kind of "shadow" president because his skills and intellect were seen as superior to those of the newly elected president.

As Kearns points out, Lincoln's other cabinet picks all had more education and government experience than the newly elected president. Of course, as we all know, Lincoln became a great leader, perhaps one of the best in American history, and his so-called team of rivals soon came to recognize his remarkable strengths. Lincoln possessed the confidence and vision to appoint strong and capable leaders to his cabinet, regardless of their previous opposition to him. He cared more about the long-term interests of the country than the potential conflict associated with surrounding himself with former rivals. Knowing he was governing in perilous times, he selected men of strength and character to serve with him and never felt insecure in his role as commander in chief.

Why do we settle for mediocrity in leadership? It's a question I have asked myself many times, particularly when I see over and over again examples of highly paid people in business, government, and the non-profits perform poorly. I can only conclude that the boards that hire and evaluate these top executives aren't looking for the qualities I admire in a leader. They haven't thought through the development of a candidate's inner leadership qualities. They don't consider true substance or assess how the candidate has managed

---

4. Doris Kearns Goodwin, *Team of Rivals: The Political Genius of Abraham Lincoln*, New York: Simon & Schuster, 2005.

crisis in the past. Résumés and references and a good interview aren't enough if what you are seeking is a straightforward leader.

Any board hiring a top leader should judge the quality of the team that leader has assembled in the past. Has he hired top-notch people who might have even greater qualifications than he does? Has he put in place a succession plan for the organization he is leaving? Has he created a true team spirit of mutual support among his current team? Does he freely give credit to others?

The higher up you rise in an organization, the less concerned you should be about getting credit. The sum total of your actions over the course of your tenure speaks louder than anything else. Harry Truman once said, "It is amazing what you can accomplish if you do not care who gets the credit." Live your life that way. Don't worry so much about who gets credit.

When I first became mayor, one of the senior members of the organization had his name on everything. From his shirts, to the office door, to the equipment, his name was ubiquitous. It signaled that he was going to get all the credit, **"Share the credit."** which would be detrimental to the people actually doing the work.

The person I hired to replace him was just the opposite. His name didn't appear on anything and he was quick to turn every achievement into something that someone else did. In fact, I could never get him to personally take credit for anything. His department was the most productive in city history. He always attributed the success to his team.

Corporate or political, it's the same. The higher up you go in the organization, the more credit you should give to others. Say less and listen more. Let other people grow in their positions and let other people have something to say. Start moving into the role of mentor. Ultimately, if your team does well, you will do well.

The quality of the people around you speaks volumes about your worth as a leader. You cannot be considered a substantive leader, regardless of your own personal knowledge of an organization, if your staff is weak. The selection of individuals of the highest caliber, whose skills in many cases may exceed your own, shows the steady self-confidence of someone who has developed a straightforward leadership style. That's the kind of leader you want to be, one whose substance shows externally but is grounded internally.

Keep Learning

It came to me while attending a Leadership Florida session in 1997 that I missed exposure to new ideas. My participation in Leadership Florida was partially motivated by my desire to engage in new issues and the experience validated that need. After five years as supervisor of elections I wasn't challenged professionally. You might relate to this. Sometimes you feel you have hit a wall in your career, that while you like your job, it's just not as mentally stimulating as you would like it to be. My learning curve had slowed considerably.

Belonging to Leadership Florida, a statewide group of people interested in the problems and solutions to public policy issues, invigorated me. I was around 49 other people, all of whom were achievers and people of varied interests. They ran businesses and non-profits or held elective office; all had something interesting to add to our meetings. Sitting in a seminar listening to a lecture, I realized how much I missed acquiring new information.

After the session, I shared my need for greater mental challenge with my husband, and told him I planned to go back to college to get a master's degree in American history. Mark had recently received his master's degree, and was aware of the challenges that a job and children presented, but he knew it would be good for me. I took only one course a semester — at night. With two young children and serving as the supervisor of elections, there was a limit.

If you don't feel challenged in your job, my solution may not be yours. For me, learning more about American history and getting an advanced degree was a longtime goal. However, there are many ways you can engage yourself in something new, be it education, a hobby, or involvement with a volunteer organization. The important thing is that you constantly learn and expand your horizons.

Going back to school was an adjustment. I had not been in school since I graduated from college in 1981. I felt awkward. All the other students were young; I was in my thirties. I wore business suits; they were in jeans. The last term paper I had written was 16 years earlier. I felt like a fish out of water. What if I didn't do well? It was a challenge, and, initially, I experienced my share of self-doubt.

Reservations aside, after the first class I was hooked. The experience did exactly what an education should do. It broadened my mind, caused me to think more analytically, and helped me become a better writer. I was focused, much more than I ever was as an undergraduate when half my focus was on having a good time. Now, with two young children, a husband, and a full-time job, I had to want to be in class.

As I immersed myself in my studies I developed a keen interest in the civil rights movement. I was introduced to historical figures like Fannie Lou Hamer, whose story is particularly inspirational. In the early 1960s, this uneducated African-American woman dared to try to register to vote in Mississippi. When she came home after her unsuccessful attempt to sign up, the owner of the plantation where she and her husband worked admonished her for even attempting to exercise this right, and warned her not to try it again. She responded, "I didn't go down there to register for you; I went down to register for myself."[5] For that, she lost her home and her job. Undaunted, she became an influential civil rights leader. Fannie Lou Hamer

---

5. Fannie Lou Hamer to Neil McMillen, "An Oral History with Fannie Lou Hamer," interview, 14 April 1972 and 25 January 1973, McCain Library and Archive, University of Southern Mississippi, Civil Rights in Mississippi Digital Archive, http://www.lib.usm.edu/~spcol/crda/oh/hamer.htm.

became a leading voice for change at the 1964 Democratic National Convention, urging the party to seat a Mississippi delegation that included African-Americans. Imagine the strength it took to take on an entrenched party establishment just two years after being denied the right to vote, and losing your home and job. Resilient and strong, Fannie Lou represented the passion of the civil rights movement.[6]

As my interest in civil rights grew, I wove my knowledge into my speeches as supervisor of elections. Putting voting rights into a historical context made my speeches more interesting. Talking about more than the nuts and bolts of running the elections process helped me to become a better communicator.

My studies also prompted me to think for the first time about running for mayor. As I learned about the civil rights movement in Tampa and the city's slow progress towards equality at the voting booth, I asked myself what I was doing to merit any mention in history. Not enough. I needed to make a more lasting difference in my own community.

Historically, East Tampa is an African-American section of Tampa. Neglected by municipal government, East Tampa had been ignored by politicians running for citywide office. Much of this neglect stemmed from the fact that African-Americans were precluded from voting in the nonpartisan Tampa municipal elections through a device known as the White Municipal Party, which instituted a white-only primary. Created in 1908, this restrictive party system remained in effect until 1947. Without African-Americans voting, it is not surprising that their neighborhoods would not receive their fair share of funding and attention. Even in more recent years, the area never received adequate investments of time or money from the city.

If I ever became mayor, I vowed to focus attention on East Tampa and to make a difference, and, as mayor, revitalizing East

---

6. Kay Mills, *This Little Light of Mine, the Story of Fannie Lou Hamer,* Lexington, KY: The University Press of Kentucky, 2007.

Tampa became one of my administration's strategic goals. We brought unprecedented private and public investment to the community, improved neighborhoods, and significantly reduced crime. One of my most cherished memories is of a group of East Tampa residents, led by activist Evangeline Best, who, when I left office, presented me with artwork depicting the East Tampa community and scrapbooks they had painstakingly made chronicling our eight years of progress. As a team we made a difference.

I have my return to education to thank for leading me down that path. Without the exposure to Tampa's civil rights history I may never have run for mayor. Even if I had, I may not have had the same focus and intensity, or the same results.

Make learning a lifetime priority. Consider going back to school to learn something new. Study what you enjoy. You may be in classes with like-minded people, and it will broaden your mind, your understanding, and your social network. A degree represents focus, dedication, and drive. You will feel better about yourself and that enhanced self-esteem will show not only in your work life but in your personal life.

"Learning leads to the best unintended consequences."

During the Great Recession, the unemployment rate topped ten percent, but was only 4.6 percent for college graduates. The high unemployment comes from those without advanced education or an area of specialization. The more educated you are, the more specialized your skills, the greater your employability.

School is not for everyone though, and people don't have to learn in a structured environment. Hobbies are terrific learning opportunities. My husband's collection of old watches has given him an enormous amount of knowledge about the relationship between watch design and cultural shifts in our country. A dear friend who collects Florida historical maps has become an authority on Florida history and the first settlers to the New World. Friends who travel extensively have acquired considerable firsthand knowledge about other cultures that can't be found in any textbook. Look at how Fannie Lou Hamer broadened her leadership and organizational abilities. She lacked a formal education, but made up for it, so to speak, with on-the-job training.

Continuous learning is essential to being a substantive leader. The power of an education and the knowledge and insights it brings is enormous. Don't underestimate its importance in your life. Our world is changing too quickly to ever stop learning. Think of the dramatic changes in health care, the financial system, and technology that have occurred in just the last several years. As a leader you have to be adept at grasping new information, internalizing what it means for your organization, and then adjusting your strategies to reflect what you have learned. It helps to be naturally inquisitive, but, more important, you have to be open to the notion that the new information and the changing landscape are relevant and essential to the continued health and growth of your organization. Keep learning and substance and credibility will follow.

The Path to Straightforward Leadership: Step 2—Substance

In this chapter I have focused on the importance of substance to being a straightforward leader. Gaining substance takes work and sacrifice. It requires that you:

- Become an authority in your field
- Learn how to communicate effectively
- Surround yourself with people of talent that may exceed your own
- Find a mentor and be willing to accept guidance and criticism from him or her and

- Acknowledge that there is always more to learn, always think long-term and be ready to gain the education or training required

The result is worth the effort.

Taken together, this means you have developed into a person capable of leading and inspiring others. Straightforward leadership means you have successfully recognized, developed, and worked to continually improve and reinforce those qualities, which are inextricably linked and reinforce one another. Whether you can comfortably wear that mantle and project straightforward leadership depends on whether you develop your inner leadership qualities and acquire the remaining three characteristics of successful leaders.

Chapter Three

———《❦》———

LEARN TO MANAGE CRISIS AND COPE WITH TRAGEDY

S
OONER OR LATER WE ALL face a crisis. Its magnitude may vary, but the need for a straightforward leader at such times is essential, and it is at such times that your leadership skills will be tested. Your ability to deal with all aspects of a crisis from communications to critical decision-making will be measured. How well you manage the crisis and yourself will add or detract from your public image and how the organization perceives you.

A calamity can take many forms. Some, like the financial disaster that engulfed Wall Street and the global economy in 2008, have sweeping ramifications. Others are isolated incidents affecting only a division in a particular organization, but to those involved it may seem just as traumatic. Crisis can result from the loss of a major customer or partner, a defective product that results in its recall, a natural disaster, or a serious ethical violation. Regardless of its source, your role as a straightforward leader is clear: keep your cool, empower your people, be present, and stay engaged. Your substance and credibility are your assets. *The relationships and trust you have built through the years and your inner leadership qualities are your strengths.* The confidence you project during a crisis to your subordinates, your peers, your industry, the community, and the media will sustain you during the toughest times.

My first test with a possible crisis occurred within minutes of being sworn in as mayor. You can imagine the joy of an inauguration. Family, friends, and supporters are gathered about in a ballroom all excited as you start your journey. Such was the atmosphere on April 1, 2003 when I took the oath of office. Festive, yes, but what I remember most was being pulled to the side of the ballroom by a very serious police captain just minutes after having delivered my first speech as mayor.

"Mayor, I've got to tell you something," Captain John Bennett said somberly. "We've gotten a very credible report from the FBI that there's a car loaded with explosives headed toward MacDill Air Force Base. We think it might be a terrorist attack."

With the memory of 9/11 less than two years old, his warning was entirely plausible. Tampa is home to MacDill Air Force Base, Central Command (CENTCOM), and U.S. Special Operations Command (SOCOM), from which the wars in Iraq and Afghanistan have been waged.

Welcome to the job of mayor.

A crisis has no schedule. Leaders must always be prepared to carry out their responsibility in a time of duress. As we talked, I created a mental checklist. Stay calm. Think through the actions that would have to be taken if the report was true. Give our police the opportunity to gather more information. Decide who I can turn to and trust. As I was new to the position as mayor, none of the staff were my own hires. I asked Bennett to keep me informed, told him that we would await further information and that I would stay close by him in the ballroom. I spent a few moments off to the side thinking through these issues. Then I rejoined the crowd of well-wishers. In my first hour as mayor I didn't give any thought to what my leadership style was, but I knew that in times of uncertainty it was best to stay calm and get all the facts.

An hour later the threat had been cleared by the FBI.

My first moments as mayor.

As mayor, I experienced several significant events concerning public safety, death, and loss. In each case, I knew people were counting on me and it was my responsibility to lead with calm confidence. During those times, I'd reflect on my core values and principles: work with others respectfully and with honesty and humility, be measured and thoughtful, admit mistakes and accept responsibility, stay positive and optimistic, and be resilient. I also drew inspiration from the stories of others who traveled dangerous journeys and prevailed.

Another source of inspiration is a poem I kept in my desk drawer, Rudyard Kipling's "If," which contains these lines:

If you can keep your head when all about you
Are losing theirs and blaming it on you;
If you can meet with Triumph and disaster
And treat those two imposters just the same;

For me, they sum up the importance of dealing positively with the inevitable valleys we encounter in life and the need to keep your wits about you. It's also important to remember that when you are in a leadership position others are looking to you for guidance and direction. Crisis — large or small — is an unavoidable part of most organizations' lifecycle, and, when they occur, their leaders must manage them in a way that leaves those around them and the entire organization stronger.

When I ran for mayor I envisioned a crisis that I might face during my tenure: a severe hurricane. For a gulf coast city with homes and businesses built right up to the bay waters, a direct hit by a severe storm would be devastating. However, I never imagined the crisis I actually faced. In my eight years as mayor, four police officers died in the line of duty. One had been assigned to accompany me to all public appearances; he was the victim of a drunk driver. Another officer was shot when he stopped a suspicious person for questioning. Two were killed during a "routine" traffic stop. The death of those two officers sparked a massive four-day manhunt for the killer. It was then, for the first time, that I saw death, despair, grief, resolve, loyalty, and resilience up close. Many people have strong leadership qualities but don't realize they have them, and, during this crisis, I saw people with untapped talents that made them true leaders. My experiences with death and crisis have altered my view of life. What I witnessed gave me a much greater understanding of loss and grief, and helped me grow as a person as well as a leader.

Straightforward leaders develop two essential qualities which helps them deal with difficult times—inner resolve and strength. They are not only important when facing public challenges, but private ones as well. A leader is not immune from personal crisis and despair, and their effects can seriously impact how you lead others.

Present, Engaged and Loyal

Mike Roberts had just been promoted to corporal. I remembered this special event because we took a picture together along with his wife Cindy and their three-year old son Adam, who was a real wiggle-worm. Mike embodied the spirit of the department. He was a "can-do" officer, full of initiative and energy, well-liked and respected. The night of his death he was patrolling the neighborhood of Sulphur Springs, a part of Tampa that has had its share of crime. A disheveled man pushing a shopping cart caught Mike's attention at around 9:30 p.m., August 19, 2009. As he questioned him, the man became violent. He wrestled with Mike, pulled out a gun, and shot him. The bullet landed underneath Mike's bulletproof vest. Ambulances and police cars filled the street; Mike's squad had rushed to the aid of their fallen comrade. Even as Mike was being taken to the hospital, everyone knew the wound was fatal.

Police Chief Stephen Hogue and I arrived at a hospital ablaze in lights. We went to the emergency room where Mike lay dead. Members of his squad were weeping by his side. I thought I understood loyalty but seeing the grief of Mike's fellow officers brought devotion to another level. The memory of one young officer, standing erect in the hospital room, stands out. Tears ran down his cheeks and it was apparent that he was having a difficult time maintaining his composure. I told him if he wanted to go somewhere and be alone for awhile I would stay with Mike. No, he replied, he would not leave his brother's side. When an officer dies, another stays with the fallen until the body is laid to rest. Officers accompany the body everywhere — to the medical examiner, to the autopsy, to the funeral home.

Being loyal and present when others are in need is an important part of being a leader. The brother and sisterhood that exists in law enforcement is something that, as mayor, I came to appreciate. Their connection goes beyond the workplace. They understand the inherent danger in their work so their commitment to support each other no matter the circumstance gives each of them a special strength.

Loyalty transforms an organization into a family and motivates members to make the organization better. In a crisis, loyalty is magnified. Law enforcement, fire rescue, and our military demonstrate how the deep bonds of loyalty encourage exceptional focus, teamwork, and leadership in chaotic situations. The September 11 tragedy is the best example of this. As first responders scrambled to understand the gravity of the situation, they quickly organized and rushed into the burning buildings to save those inside. Sadly, the collapse of the buildings brought death to hundreds of firefighters, police, and emergency workers. They will always be remembered for their heroic teamwork, as they bravely worked together in an uncertain and tumultuous atmosphere. The strength of the team, mutual trust, and loyalty empowered them to be their best during a crisis no one could have imagined.

"Loyalty transforms an organization into a family."

It took a while to bring Cindy, who lived in the next county, to the hospital. Chief Hogue and I met her at the emergency room entrance. Later she said she knew her husband had passed as soon as she saw me. The mayor wouldn't have been there unless it was a catastrophe. Mike Roberts was an important part of our team. The loss shook us all to the core.

Tragedy struck again on June 29, 2010. The phone rang at 2:45 a.m.

Most people become alarmed at late-night calls. As mayor, I never looked forward to calls from the police chief at any time. When I answered the phone, it was Chief Hogue's successor, Jane Castor.

Her voice was flat. I knew what was coming.

"Mayor, two police officers on a routine traffic stop were both shot in the head. One is dead and the other is in critical condition." I collected my thoughts for a minute. Both shot in the head? How could that happen? Could there be a mistake? My mind flashed to the image of Corporal Roberts on the emergency room table. Sorrow swept over me as I anticipated the heartache that lay ahead. I woke my husband, Mark, and told him the news. Along deserted roads at 3:00 a.m., I again made the drive to Tampa General Hospital, this time wondering who was behind such a violent act. At the hospital, hundreds of distraught officers lined the hallways, displaying a mixture of stoicism and shock. With a different police chief,

I made the all-too-familiar walk through the bright lights of the hospital hallways to the emergency room.

Both officers were 31 years old. I went first to see Jeff Kocab, who had been pronounced dead at the hospital. Only six months earlier Jeff had been in my office for the Christmas open house. We took a photo together and I kidded him, saying, "You're too young to be a police officer."

Dave Curtis was in the adjoining room. Doctors and nurses hovered over him working with quiet determination. Dave was a big man who exercised regularly and loved sports and the outdoors. Now he was clinging to life.

It was hard to believe this was the result of a routine traffic stop. A woman, Cortnee Brantley, was driving a car without a license tag. Officer Curtis pulled her over. Sitting in the passenger seat was a man named Dontae Morris. Dave asked Brantley for her driver's license and registration and he asked the passenger his name.

"Dontae Morris," he said, the dash cam video in the police car picking up the exchange.

Officer Curtis wrote the name on his pad, then went back to his police cruiser and ran the names through the squad car's computer, which revealed an outstanding warrant for Morris's arrest for something relatively minor—a bad check.

Dave called for backup and Jeff responded. They did everything by the book.

They approached the car on Morris's side.

"What's the deal with your warrant? Do you know anything about it?" Curtis asked Morris as the video recorder captured their interaction.

Officer Curtis told Morris to step out of the car and put his hands behind his back. In one swift movement, Morris turned and shot both officers. It was over in an instant.

Morris took off running, Brantley squealed off in her vehicle.

What the two officers didn't know was that Morris had recently been released from prison and had been questioned about another murder since then. A traffic stop turned nightmare.

Officers were dispatched to bring both men's wives to the hospital, as both lived more than an hour away. While we waited, the chief told me that Jeff's wife was nine months' pregnant and that Kelly and Dave had four boys all under the age of nine, the youngest only eight months old.

"Can it get any worse than this?" I wondered. One officer dead; another close to death, both highly respected, loved by their families, friends, and fellow police officers. Words can never adequately describe those early morning hours.

The role of the leader in a time of overwhelming grief is to be present, engaged, and loyal. The chief and I were there to help others. Sometime around 5 a.m., Sara Kocab and Kelly Curtis, the officers' wives, arrived and we escorted them down the hospital corridors, lined with officers, to their husbands' side. For the rest of those early morning hours, I stayed with Jeff and Dave.

At 6:00 a.m., about three hours after the shootings, Chief Castor and I walked out into the oppressive humidity of a summer morning to a bank of television cameras and reporters gathered on the hospital grounds, and announced that Jeff had died and that Dave was near death. He died later that morning.

An inter-agency operations command center was established near the murder scene. It was led by the Tampa Police Department (TPD) and supported by the Hillsborough County Sheriff's Office, the Secret Service, the FBI, even the Florida Fish and Wildlife Services. After we left the hospital, the chief and I went there.

Because we had the video and knew who the killer was, his speedy capture seemed a foregone conclusion. When Corporal Roberts was killed, the police caught the murderer within an hour. I thought Morris would be captured quickly. He wasn't.

He wasn't captured that day.

He wasn't captured the next day. Or the day after that.

A manhunt such as this became was unprecedented in Tampa and gripped our community. Although we had experienced the tragic death of an officer before, we had not experienced the emotional intensity of a prolonged search for a killer. Dontae Morris was still at-large, and the search for this killer enveloped our community and tested all of those involved for four days.

Tampa is a community that cares deeply about police officers, firefighters, and our military. Perhaps because we have many active and retired military residents, we have a strong collective sense of respect for those who protect the lives of others. Now we had not only lost two of our finest police officers, but the murderer was on the loose—armed and dangerous. For the next four days I spent most of my time at the command center.

Hot, muggy, tense. The command center expanded day by day as more law enforcement agencies joined in the hunt. There were SWAT teams, canine units, and law enforcement officers from across the state helping in the search. Although the TPD led the manhunt, there were no inter-agency squabbles, no clash of egos— just a determined group of dedicated law enforcement personnel working together on the singular mission: find the killer. They were a family, loyal to their fallen brothers, determined to find the person responsible. Tents were set up in the parking lot of the command center; food by the truckload was delivered by area restaurants and citizens who just wanted to help. The outpouring of community support was tremendous. The "family" had expanded.

Assistant Chief John Bennett (previously Captain Bennett from my first hour as mayor), was in charge of operations. There was no one better for the job. Serious and dedicated, Bennett is a detail man. There wasn't a lead that   "One Team" he wouldn't follow all the way to the end. Finding Morris turned out to be a lot harder than we thought. A $100,000 reward for information leading to Morris's arrest and conviction was posted. The leads poured in. One minute rumors had Morris in Jacksonville, the next minute he was in Miami. At the end of the third day, Bennett told me they had located a confidential informant whose information seemed to have merit. Chief Castor and I shared a growing concern that capturing Morris would not be without more violence. He had little to lose and we feared he would shoot another officer or that a member of the public might unwittingly cross paths with him. Our anxiety grew each day.

The funeral for the two officers was approaching. I was to deliver one of the eulogies, and found it impossible to write. I dreaded that Morris might not be caught before the funeral and the effect that would have on the families and our entire police department. The night before the funeral, the eulogies were still unwritten. Tired, I vowed to get up early in the morning and write them before leaving for the service. At 10 p.m., the chief called to say the words I had been waiting to hear: Morris had been captured. As my husband and I drove to the police station, the weight of the past four days began to lift. The focus and intensity paid off. The killer had been taken into custody and the community could feel safe again. We could lay our officers to rest knowing their killer was behind bars.

The plaza outside the police station was flooded in light from the television cameras. In front of the police station is the memorial on which the names of officers killed in the line of duty are engraved in granite. Just the day before, the chief and I had participated in a solemn ceremony during which the names of Officers Kocab and Curtis were engraved. The monument was overflowing with flowers and notes that hundreds of visitors had left. Assistant Chief Bennett, who had played such a pivotal role in the manhunt, stood next to me quietly. I thanked him for his leadership, and he, like all good leaders, said it was about the team.

I returned home at about midnight, finally able to think clearly about what I wanted to say. The words poured out as I wrote the eulogies for Jeff and Dave. Morris's capture allowed us to focus solely on honoring the fallen men. Their families had a long emotional journey ahead, but this was one important step toward closure.

As I look back on those four days, I am proud of the after-action report of an outside, independent firm that analyzed the events and evaluated the performance of our police department.[7] The report complimented the department on the way the search was conducted. It found a strong relationship had been established between the community and the police department and that this relationship aided the effort. Our police department had established its credentials well before the crisis, and the substance and credibility of the chief and the entire department made for effective leadership when it was most needed.

In the aftermath, Chief Castor and I received many spontaneous heartfelt comments from the community. We were both ill at ease with the accolades. We felt we were just doing our jobs. We didn't think we were setting some great example of leadership. Leaders view their work as doing what is expected, not as exceptional.

Being present in a crisis is vital. Being in the midst of the action is a big part of leadership. In a crisis the straightforward leader is always present, engaged, and loyal. There is no substitute for the person at the top knowing the details, absorbing the big picture, and providing strength to the people performing their work. The leader becomes one with the team.

---

7. James K. Stewart, Denise Rodriguez King, and Ron Lafond, *Tampa Bay Manhunt After Action Report: Lessons Learned in Community Police Partnerships & Incident Command System*, CAN Analysis Solutions, 2011. The report can be downloaded at http://www.cna.org/research/2011/tampa-bay-manhunt-after-action-report. CNA is an independent, non-profit organization; funding for the report came from the Office of Community Oriented Policing Services (COPS), and the U.S. Department of Justice.

It was essential for me to be at the hospital with the fallen officers and the larger family of officers. Maybe there was nothing I could say, but I had to be there. My daily presence at the command center during the search was imperative. It let the police know we were in this together, side by side. We would not falter. The mission was going to be completed. The chief and I were a team, working together at all times. It was essential that the chief and I communicate to the public, be there when the killer was caught, and be with the families at the funeral. When you are in a leadership position, there is no substitute for simply being there in a crisis. Your presence and demeanor matter.

When a crisis affects what is close to you, engagement comes naturally. After seven years as mayor, I had formed a bond with the police. We had weathered tragedy before. I respected the work they did in our community. I had also grown to love Tampa in a way I hadn't before I became mayor. I knew every neighborhood and the wonderful mix of people who call Tampa home. Protecting our city and citizens against harm was a responsibility I carried every day.

When you and the organization you lead become one, you have internalized the role of leader beyond the title or the job description. When you truly love your company and feel a sense of responsibility for the people who work with you, you become a very different kind of leader than one who is simply doing his job. You develop an emotional attachment to the organization and a keen sense of ownership. Being present and engaged in a crisis is the natural response of a leader who is emotionally invested in the organization he leads. *The straightforward leader must care deeply.*

The 9/11 attacks on New York City are an excellent example of executive leadership during a crisis. As the twin towers at the World Trade Center (WTC) collapsed Mayor Giuliani was right in the thick of the action, running down the street through shattered glass and debris, grabbing reporters along the way in order to quickly get information out to the public. Initially, he had to make decisions in a vacuum because he did not know the full extent of the crisis.

They had to set up a command center—the city's command center located at the WTC had been destroyed—and quickly figure out the best way to communicate to the public. Throughout the first few days, Giuliani held press conferences and spoke eloquently to the city and the nation about the crisis. He was authoritative but also an emotional New Yorker and American. His actions are a case study in effective, engaged leadership during a crisis.

On the flip side is the mayor of New Orleans during Hurricane Katrina. He seemed out of touch, lacking authority, and, rather than take responsibility, he blamed state and federal authorities for not providing needed help. The state and the federal governments may well have failed in their duties, but the mayor broke the cardinal rule of leadership: take responsibility. As the person tasked with protecting his citizens, he should have been in the thick of things. If people were stuck in the Louisiana Superdome, then, the mayor needed to personally figure out a way to get them needed supplies or move them to another location. His actions are a case study in poor leadership.

The importance of a present and engaged leader was drilled into me at an early age. Florida 1974. Court-ordered busing to achieve racial integration was an emotional issue in Florida in the early 1970s. Often students had to be bused out of their neighborhoods to schools in other districts. This was the second year of the busing. I was in the ninth grade, and, at my junior high, busing combined with middle school hormones and summer heat was a combustible mixture.

I won a race for student council president in that environment and so was in a leadership position during a time of great unrest. One day, at lunchtime, a race riot started. It began with name-calling and escalated into physical violence. Students left their classrooms and filled the hallways. It was dangerous to be in a bathroom where you could be pushed around or worse. The situation was volatile.

As president of the student council I went to the main office to see what, if any, role I could play. I have never forgotten the principal, who stayed in his office and didn't come out to address the students or try to quiet the situation. Even at 15, I thought this was wrong. This was an extreme situation and it required leadership. Still, the principal hid, not using his power as the head of the school to calm and control the situation.

As parents found out what was going on—this was long before cell phones and texting—they called the school and arrived in droves to take their kids home. It was bedlam. The police arrived and restored order and, for the rest of the school year, sheriff's deputies policed the school.

I took away a valuable lesson in leadership.

Let Good People Lead

My confidence during the manhunt was bolstered by the knowledge that Jane Castor was a straightforward leader. I had appointed her chief of police in September 2009 when Chief Hogue retired. He had been grooming her as his successor so I was able to carefully evaluate her performance as assistant chief. For 26 years she had steadily risen in the ranks of the police department, holding almost every position. When I appointed her, I felt she would be a worthy successor to Chief Hogue. She was the first female police chief in the city of Tampa, but, as she said at the time, she just wanted to be known as a first-rate chief. She turned out to be more than that. She was a great leader.

Chief Castor is six-foot one-inches tall, slim, and a former college basketball player. She is also the mother of two boys and comes from a large, close-knit family. Well-balanced and funny, she had earned the respect of her fellow officers.

The Chief and I became a team during that crisis. We had been together in the hospital with the families and together we poured the necessary resources into finding the killer. Together we helped one another perform at a high level. We were a team and that's what the public saw.

A leader must decide who the face of a crisis will be. Sometimes it is the mayor, the governor, the CEO. Sometimes it is the police chief, the head of emergency operations, or a technical person well-versed in the specifics of the emergency. Each case is different, but a leader must decide who the first to the microphone is. The best face of a crisis may not always be the person at the top of the organizational chart. After observing Castor in the first day of the crisis, I decided she should be the go-to person. She could communicate more effectively about the investigation, the reward money, confidential informants, and tactics. I was mayor, but Castor was the best person to be front and center during this crisis. She was an effective communicator, she knew the details, and she was credible.

When a killer is on the loose, the public has a right to know what is being done. They are fearful and can't be kept in the dark. We held several press conferences each day although we didn't always have a lot of progress to report. Press conferences gave the chief an opportunity to let anyone within earshot of a radio, television, or the Internet know that if they were harboring Morris, they would be held accountable. It gave us an opportunity to talk about the reward money and encourage people to come forward. It also provided us the opportunity to convey to the community the intensity of the manhunt.

> "Let your people lead."

By the Chief's side, I provided support and ensured that the tone of dogged determination and ultimate success was consistently conveyed. There was never a doubt in my mind that we would find Morris. I knew the quality of the people involved. Good people were leading. We were an effective team and, in times of crisis, the public wants to see unity of effort and commitment on the part of their leaders.

Each situation is different. If the threat had been a natural disaster, a bomb explosion, terrorist attack, or similar calamity, I would have been the face. The overall severity of the event and potential scope of the impact to the community determines who the go-to person should be. In those situations, you must operate on many different levels, moving from an operational level of coordination and organization, to an emotional level of connecting with the community and offering direction or comfort. In 2004 we faced the threat of a fast moving Hurricane Charley, which was expected to directly hit Tampa Bay. I was constantly on the television and radio preparing our residents for this Category 4 storm. In fact, I was doing a live television interview when the station's weatherman told me on air that the hurricane had turned to the east and would miss Tampa altogether.

During the BP oil spill disaster, someone at BP decided that their CEO, Tony Hayward, was the face of the disaster. It was a terrible error. He may have been at the top of the organizational chart, but he lacked the skills to be the face of the company during the crisis. He appeared weak and testy, and he certainly flunked the leadership test when he lamented publicly that "he wanted his life back." In a crisis, it is always about the crisis and its effect on others, never about the person in charge.

The company, and Hayward, should have been confident enough in their team to have calmly evaluated who the best spokesman should be. The crisis occurred in the United States — maybe an American would be a better spokesman than an Englishman. The crisis was affecting people of relatively modest means who made their living from fishing or in the tourism industry. The face of BP needed to be someone who could easily relate to those people who were in so much distress. BP chose a CEO who didn't have a complete leader personality. He performed adequately until a crisis occurred, and then his weakness as a leader came through loud and clear.

The manhunt for the killer of our police officers was a highly focused effort led by experts in law enforcement. The entire operation was a lesson in the value of extremely focused quality people; all the people and agencies involved were intent on the mission. Chief

Castor made my job easier. She allowed others to do their jobs and made sure the team received all the credit. From my point of view, it was a time to let other straightforward leaders demonstrate their abilities.

When you have high-quality people in your organization, let them lead when the time comes. Select superior people and let them perform. Ultimately, it reflects well on the entire organization.

Do the "Next Thing" to Manage Grief

When I became mayor, I didn't want a police officer to watch over me and I didn't want a Lincoln Continental—two things assigned to me upon taking office. Both were a tradition of the mayor's office and, reluctantly, I accepted both.

Detective Juan Serrano was assigned as my "bodyguard," for lack of a better term. Chief Hogue thought Juan would be a good fit. I fussed because it seemed intrusive and I didn't believe I needed any protection. However, Hogue insisted that I have someone with me during public appearances and I had to trust his judgment. I relented, and Juan accompanied me to events.

As mayor I attended a great many events, sometimes seven in one day. Juan was quiet and very attentive to everything around him. A native of Puerto Rico, Juan was a 20-year veteran with the Tampa Police Department and had special training in dignitary protection. At first I bristled at having someone with me for so many hours, but, soon, Juan and I started talking and began to trust one another. I'm a talker and after each event the conversation flowed. Juan became a close friend. He was the consummate professional and I knew he had my best interests at heart.

As the years went by, our trust in one another grew. No matter what I said to him, I knew it wouldn't go any further and he felt the same way. We shared our hopes, dreams, and aspirations. Sometimes we shared embarrassing moments, like the time I showed up at the wrong funeral service, causing quite a stir with the bereaved family who couldn't believe I had come to honor their family member. He accompanied me and my family on a Panama trade mission, coordinating the trip with Panamanian officials down to the last detail. We had formed a strong bond.

Every year Tampa hosts one of the most prestigious running events in the country, the Gasparilla Distance Classic. One of my goals was to run the entire 5K rather than walk most of it as I had been doing. I trained and was determined to finish with a respectable time. February 25, 2006, was race day. It was a beautiful winter day. A lovely blue sky and crisp air awaited thousand of runners. I trotted along, slower probably than most walkers, but when I ran across the finish line the first person I saw was Juan giving me a thumbs-up. We were slow getting out of the course. Dozens of participants and spectators wanted pictures with me—having your picture taken is part of a mayor's job description. Finally we broke free, and Juan dropped me off at home.

"Thanks, Juan, it was a great day," I said. "See you Monday." But I didn't see Juan on Monday. As Juan was ending his shift and driving home, he was struck and killed by a drunk driver.

Chief Hogue called to tell me Juan had been in an auto accident; he didn't know then if it was serious. My first thought was that it couldn't be too bad because Juan was such a careful driver. My husband, Mark, and I drove to Tampa General Hospital, thinking all the way how upset Juan was going to be if he had a broken bone or was incapacitated in any way. I will never forget the look on the ER doctor's face when he told us Juan had died. I didn't believe his words until I went in to see Juan myself. Only then did I believe that my friend was truly gone. Mark and I were devastated. We all experience the loss of family members, friends, and colleagues. Dealing with death and the accompanying emotions when you are in a high-profile public position is a challenge that I faced and ultimately found a way to work through.

On Monday, Chief Hogue held a press conference to talk about the death of his officer in the line of duty and asked me to speak. I burst into tears. Right in front of a whole bank of cameras, with every local newspaper, radio, and television station there. I couldn't stop myself; it was a big cry. How terrible to have broken down in public! I felt like a loser for crying—as mayor I should have been able to hold my emotions in check and speak about Juan. I felt that I had not represented the office or the people of Tampa well.

Nevertheless, this experience taught me something about showing emotion. Police officers told me my tears helped them mourn. They were positive and supportive. It was important to them to know how much I cared and it was okay for them to grieve outwardly too. Those in leadership positions may be reluctant to show emotion, but sometimes they should. I cried many times during my eight years as mayor and have learned that there is nothing wrong with showing authentic emotion.

Juan's funeral was a formal, line-of-duty service because he died returning from his watch with me. It was emotional and heart wrenching to see Juan's many friends and loving family.

I lost my trusted friend.

My parents knew Juan, too. He was a member of our extended family. At the funeral, my father sat just one seat away from me. Normally robust and in good health, on that day he did not look well. It turned out his kidneys hadn't been working well for three days. He was part of the World War II generation—those who don't complain until it's too late.

From that February day, it was downhill for my father.

The ultimate diagnosis came a few months later: bladder cancer. It had metastasized, and the prognosis was very grim. Even so, he wanted to try chemotherapy despite the low probability for success. The chemotherapy only made him weaker. That October, he had a debilitating stroke.

My father was a man full of life who dominated the stage for most of his 82 years. Born in Italy, his family immigrated to the United States when he was two. After serving as a paratrooper in World War II, including the Battle of the Bulge, the GI Bill allowed him the opportunity to receive an education and he became a college professor. He was a true Renaissance man, good at many things, an intellectual who could relate to every person, and beloved by his students. My father and I were close. We talked at great length about many topics and I always came away feeling wiser. He instilled in me the importance of living a life of integrity and setting high standards for oneself. He was the best possible father.

From Juan's funeral until my father's death in February 2007, I watched him decline and suffer. I was in a state of despair—a part of the large family of people who have lost a loved one from cancer. All you have to say is "My dad died of cancer," and the rest of the story is sadly understood.

For the first time in my life I didn't want to face the day. I've always been an early riser, getting up without an alarm clock between 5:30 and 6 a.m. I looked forward to the beginning of every day. But now, I needed an alarm clock to rouse me. During this time I kept a full schedule as mayor, raised our two high school-aged children and ran for re-election. There's no avoiding the day when you are the mayor or a parent.

My despair had two sources. One was watching my father deteriorate. His misery was hard to accept. After my father died, the heaviness began to lift. I could accept his death because his suffering was over. The other source of my despondency was my belief that I was partially responsible for Juan's death. I could not shake the feeling that, if not for me, Juan would still be alive. Juan had a full life and many plans for the future.

If I hadn't run in the Gasparilla Classic 5K, I thought, he would still be alive. I didn't have to run; the previous mayor never participated in any of the races. I could have participated in the opening ceremony and gone home, or not attended at all. I thought about those photos I stopped to take, and the extra time I spent chatting with everybody. If I hadn't done those things, Juan would not have been in the path of the drunk driver.

Of course, I knew that accidents were random and that the person responsible for Juan's death was the drunk driver who came over the hill. My rational mind understood all of that, but the mind is complex and the process of grief and understanding tragedy and its place in your life takes time to digest and to come to terms with. It can't be dismissed just because your logical side tells you it should.

My demeanor must have conveyed how I felt because I received a lovely phone call from Juan's widow Mylin, who wanted me to know that I shouldn't feel responsible, that it was meant to be. She was very kind to reach out. Still, the thoughts persist, and even now I carry the memory of Juan's death with me. I continue to go to the Gasparilla race every year. It's a way to pay tribute to him. It is not easy to lead when you are travelling a difficult emotional journey. I learned a great lesson about grief and despair and how to continue to lead because in a high profile position others look to you for daily guidance, so you have to go on.

As mayor your life is all about the schedule. It starts in the morning and it ends at night. Everything is public; you are always interacting with people. There is no downtime until you get home. There are meetings, endless speeches and presentations, ceremonial events and lots of photos. Having an off day is not an option because the speech you delivered that day might be the only impression someone gets of you, and the city. The appointment in your office could be someone who has waited months for face time. Even in the grocery store, it's about greeting people and listening to their concerns.

In addition, our two children were in high school and they required time and attention. Life had to go on, and I had to figure out a way to keep functioning at a high level. Falling apart was not an option. Staying at home was not possible, I had too much responsibility.

What worked for me and allowed me to continue to fulfill my responsibilities to the city and to my family was to "do the next thing." This may sound simplistic, but it worked. The next thing didn't mean the next scheduled appointment on my calendar at work. It meant getting out of bed, making breakfast, reading the paper, getting the kids off to school, making a phone call—taking the next step to the next step. I made a list of each step so I could cross my accomplishments off the list. I focused my day on the next item on the list. The act of writing down and then crossing off everything I was to do gave me the emotional energy to make it to the next item on the list. Since childhood I have always needed a plan, and this was the plan. At the end of the day, I could look at the list, see every item crossed off, and feel that I had made it. The next day it would start over. It was my way to cope, to lead myself out of despondency.

Though not everyone is in a high profile leadership position, we all have to lead ourselves. Grief strikes each of us; no one is immune. Everyone has problems at some point in their lives—some are more severe or more frequent than others. The effects of grief are pervasive and can make it impossible to work or have positive relationships.

Many people don't see themselves as leaders, particularly if they are not in a professional environment and don't have a title. What they don't realize is that leadership takes many forms and one of them is leading yourself and your family. I have close friends who have lost children through terrible tragedies. As they make their way forward, they may not recognize in themselves what I do: their leadership. They are resilient; they do the "next thing" to manage their own grief and provide guidance for their families.

> "To get through difficult times, do the next thing."

When we see parts of our country devastated by tornadoes or floods, what do people do the day after the storm? They do the next thing, whatever is necessary to get through the day. When crisis strikes, if you do a little bit more each day, you will start to see progress. Do what needs to be done, item by item, and take a moment to say, "Look what I've accomplished." You have a right to be proud of even small accomplishments.

Isn't that really the key to moving forward in life, doing the next thing? Making a list speaks to how most problems are overcome — one step at a time. Most people don't solve problems in big chunks, they do it step-by-step. It is often a slow and incremental process. Don't be concerned if it takes a very long time to work through a difficult period in your life. There is no "right" amount of time; it varies for each of us. Grief may even change you as a person, and change is also an evolutionary process. Take each small step and stop occasionally to see how far you have come.

While my father was dying, I was running for a second term. The election was in March. My father died that February. I must have run the worst re-election campaign in history. I paid little attention to it; my priorities were elsewhere. Nevertheless, I was re-elected with 79 percent of the vote. As you might imagine, I was extra appreciative of all of my friends and supporters who helped during that dark time. I survived this terrible experience and I'm stronger for it. I became a more empathetic person and I have a better understanding of life.

As mayor, I attended many funerals of friends, acquaintances, and people who contributed to the community. I always listened closely to the eulogies to ensure I understood, as best I could, the totality of the life we were celebrating. It helped me understand that a good and meaningful life is composed of two things: (1) having a family whom they loved and who loved them (My definition of family is very broad.), and (2) giving more than you receive. When a person is a giver—emotionally, spiritually, and (if they happen to have money) monetarily—we can truly celebrate their life.

I remember my last moments with my father. Under the care of hospice, he was in his den surrounded by his many books, his art, and the music he loved. It was a beautiful, brisk February day and as a cool breeze filled the room where he lay and lifted his soul away, it was really just about our relationship—his, my mother's, and mine—as a family.

We should all live our lives in preparation for that final moment and concentrate on the important things: our family, our relationships, our contributions to others. I think back on the deaths of Corporal Roberts, Officers Jeff Kocab and Dave Curtis and the tremendous leadership their wives, Cindy, Sara, and Kelly, demonstrated. They, too, did the next thing, and their resiliency and courage were a lesson and inspiration.

Cindy trained and rode in the Police Unity Tour, a national, three-day bicycle ride. She raises her son, Adam, she always participates in events that recognize her husband's sacrifice and she attends each court appearance of his killer.

Kelly was suddenly a widow with four young boys to rear. She consistently handled herself with grace and strength during the time of the tragedy and afterwards. She trained and ran in our annual Police Memorial 5K a year after Dave's death. She and Sara Kocab have formed a bond and are supportive of one another.

Sara was nine months pregnant at the time of Jeff's death. Several weeks later she gave birth to a stillborn child she and Jeff had already named Lilly. Chief Castor and I visited her in the hospital. How drained and overcome she must have been. The next morning Dontae Morris was scheduled to be arraigned. Sara said she planned to be there to face the man who took her husband's life. I didn't think it possible.

The next morning Kelly accompanied Sara. They sat in the front row of the courtroom while Morris appeared before the judge. It was an incredible moment that spoke to the resiliency of these two women. They would be loyal to the memory and sacrifice of their fallen husbands and see that justice was served. As of this writing, Dontae Morris is in jail awaiting trial.

Sometimes we all get a little low and wonder how we can keep going. I hope you think about Sara, Kelly, and Cindy or someone you know the next time you get knocked down and doubt you can get back up. Dig deep and find that resilient spirit inside of you. I have seen it firsthand and will never forget it. Then, do the next thing; take small steps and you will find that you have travelled a considerable distance.

The Path to Straightforward Leadership:
Step 3—Managing Crisis and Coping with Tragedy

In this chapter, I have focused on the importance of being there in the face of crisis and of taking the next step when faced with tragedy in your personal or professional life. Neither is easy.

When times demand it, crisis requires that you:

- Find the strength that adversity brings out in you
- Be present—physically and emotionally—be engaged, and be loyal
- Work as a team, always as one
- Let the good people on your team lead when the situation requires their leadership

In times of grief, it is even more important that we stand by one another. When personal grief strikes you, take one step at a time, and do the next thing. It will help you manage yourself so you can continue to lead yourself and others.

Chapter Four

———⟨ⰟⰟ⟩———

CHANGE HAS CHANGED

WHY IS THE TOPIC OF change so important today and regularly mentioned as integral to business and organizational success? After all, we have always lived with change. It is a natural and fundamental part of growth for businesses and human beings alike. We celebrate the milestones of aging as we grow from an infant to toddler, from toddler to teenager, from teenager to young adult, and beyond. Founding Father Benjamin Franklin noted, "When you're finished changing, you're finished." He knew a thing or two about change; his 84 years encompassed two revolutions—the American and French that radically altered the global landscape.

Change is about making something different from what it was before. You change your career, your hairstyle, your attitude, your diet. Change has always been an essential part of living. However, in the 21st Century even change has changed because of the speed at which it occurs. To illustrate what I mean, let's compare what were once new forms of communication: the telephone and the Internet. Both were transformative, yet they travelled very different paths as they were refined and came into popular use. One was a change that occurred in what might be called the age of change; the other occurred on the cusp of a new era in which the very nature of change had changed.

In 1876, inventor Alexander Graham Bell uttered the words, "Mr. Watson, come here; I want to see you," to his assistant into an experimental device, later called the telephone. Communication would never be the same. From the time of its invention, the technology surrounding the telephone *steadily* progressed. In order to have a telephone system, a mechanism had to be developed to connect thousands of phone lines to one another. In 1878, a switchboard system, which connected many lines through a single exchange, was designed. Each call was manually handled by operators, so the switchboard centers were a beehive of activity as operators scrambled to connect an ever growing number of calls. In 1889, the invention of the "Strowger Switch" allowed one line to connect to as many as 100 lines. The development of the telephone grew throughout the early 20th Century, with the advent of more advanced switchboards, underground cables, long-distance lines, and a cooperative exchange for farmers. By 1948, there were 30 million phones in use in the United States.

The switchboard method of telephone transmission predominated until automatic switching technology came into widespread use in the middle of the twentieth century. You may remember the 1960s television series, the "Andy Griffith Show," with Sheriff Andy Taylor and Deputy Barney Fife. Whenever they made a telephone call, they rang up "Sarah" and asked to be connected to another party. Because "Sarah" was a switchboard operator; they were actually still using a system first developed in the late 1800s. The telephone was a transformative invention yet one that evolved slowly. From its inception to present day telephone technology, it took nearly 80 years.

In the second half of the 20th Century a new form of communication was developed. In 1969, the Internet, known as ARPANET, connected four major universities. When the researchers at UCLA tried to send their first message, "LOGIN," from one computer to another, the transmission failed when they got to the "G." Nonetheless, a connection had been established.

The ARPANET was seen as an alternative form of communication for the military. It was not envisioned as something for commercial or personal use. That didn't last long. E-mail was developed in 1972, and the speed of data transfer was increased using a T-3 line in the late 1980s. The World Wide Web, created in 1989 and introduced to the public in 1991, tremendously expanded the use of the Internet, as it was then called. Search engines were developed to help organize the vast amount of information available on the web. By the mid 1990s the Internet was firmly established as the new way to communicate across the globe. From inception to its modern day use: 30 years.

In 1965, Gordon Moore, the co-founder of Intel, noted that the transistor count on integrated circuit boards had doubled roughly every two years, a trend he expected to continue until about 2020. Moore's prediction (known as Moore's Law) has not only been on point but is often credited with spurring the IT industry to develop new processors and expand computer capabilities about every eighteen months. Rapid technological change has become a given, and the expectation of more processing power has sparked ever more technological innovation. In turn, lower costs of production have made technology more accessible to the average person prompting societal changes that previous generations could not have imagined.

Change has changed? Change is no longer a plodding, predictable driving force; it is ubiquitous and unpredictable. It has resulted in the Internet, social media, the almost instantaneous transmission of information, rapid technological advances, and the availability of advanced technology for Americans of vastly different lifestyles and economic status.

Change is about getting the job done even as new circumstances arise. It is a way of seeing the next day, the future, as something better than it was the day before. As parents thinking about the development of our children, we focus on the next day, the next year, and the next decade. Our focus on their future is a form of leadership. How can our children progress from one level to the next if we stay fixated on the past?

The same is true when you think about your organization. If the people in your organization spend their time lamenting how things used to be, they lack an important component of leadership: a future orientation. The future and change are positive and not to be feared. Holding on to how things are done today or have been done in the past makes no more sense than holding your children to elementary school standards when they have progressed to high school. The new norm of rapid change is dynamic and exciting. This century is filled with possibilities that can strengthen organizations and societies.

This change in change makes the role of the straightforward leader even more important. You cannot usher in this fast-paced transformation without bringing people along; individuals must understand the need for change in order to embrace it. A straightforward leader understands that change won't stick if people aren't part of the process and haven't been properly prepared. It starts with a vision, gets translated to your employees and to your customers, or constituents. Change is simply getting the job done, albeit in a different way, using different tools, methods, approaches, and technologies.

As a straightforward leader, you can effectively lead change when you:

- *Understand that change has changed:* The vision of change embraces the reality of the 21st Century; rapid and never-ending change that gets the job done in a better way.

- *Establish the vision, mission, and goals of the organization:* Taking the time to chart your direction and prepare your team keeps the focus on the change priorities.

- *Motivate your existing team and recruit new talent:* Quality people want to belong to an organization that has clearly established goals and is making a difference.

- *Listen to all sides and involve affected stakeholders:* A true leader isn't heavy-handed in pushing change. Effective and lasting change comes about through consensus and understanding.

- *Choose your change battles carefully:* Your strategic goals help guide your decisions about which change to accomplish first and where the benefits of change outweigh the organization's disruption.

- *Embrace technological advances:* New technology can mean expansion and growth; therefore, it is vital to understand the next new thing and how it can be applied to your organization.

Inner leadership qualities are key to building the rapport needed to effectuate change. An effective change agent communicates with credibility. The straight-forward leader anticipates and channels the inevitability of change so that those who follow them make a deliberate decision to improve and are empowered to do so. The management team, employees, customers, shareholders, constituents, and contributors are active participants, not spectators subject to forces beyond their control, on the path toward improvement.

When a board of directors or some other outside force has to tell and direct the person at the top to guide change, there is a problem. The straightforward leader doesn't need to be told; he is able to identify trends early, devise a plan, communicate effectively, and bring a different, better way of doing business to his organization. He treats change as a reality, an ally, not something to resist. He thinks of unique and different ways to change, and does not wait for it to be thrust upon him or the organization. This leader understands that change has changed and we are not operating in an earlier paradigm. There is no wistful thinking about how things used to be, no sentimentality for the past. The straightforward leader visualizes an exciting future as an opportunity to advance, to bring a company from second place to first, fueled by new ideas and different ways to get the job done. It is realistic optimism at its best.

Directing Change

How well I remember my first meeting of the State Association of Supervisors of Elections in 1993. I had just been elected supervisor of elections for Hillsborough County after serving two terms on the County Commission. At age 34, I was eager for this new challenge — my first opportunity to run my own organization. I had lots of ideas about how to improve the election process and my enthusiasm showed. For my fellow supervisors, it was not love at first sight. They were mostly older than I, and a majority from smaller, rural counties. Many had grown up in their respective offices, starting in a lesser position and gradually working themselves up until they were ready to run for the top elected job. You only earned their respect after successfully running a general election and understanding how difficult administering an election can be. This group did not embrace change easily, and my ideas for change fell flat. An elderly, veteran supervisor from the Panhandle of Florida came up and wagged her finger at me, "Ain't nothin' ever gonna change. The way it is, is the way it is. So don't try changing anything."

Well, that pretty much said it all. Tread carefully!

Actually, she did me a favor by letting me know that in her view there was no need to promote change. Better for me to understand this from the start than to act like a bull in a china shop. She made it very clear that my ideas would not be well received. I am sure my judgmental attitude towards my new profession did not go undetected either. What were my credentials? What made me credible?

The fact is, at that point in my career, I could not effectively direct change. I had not yet earned the respect of my peers, nor did I have the necessary experience and knowledge to develop a plan for change. Respect is earned. With no experience in the field of elections, any thoughts I had about change carried little weight with my colleagues.

Now, fast forward seven years to the period following the 2000 presidential election and the election reform initiative that followed. My presentation to the Election Reform Commission in Tallahassee, as president of the State Association of Supervisors of Elections, became the foundation for statewide changes. Why? My long-term performance as an elections official had earned me the right to present my ideas for change. After laying out the predicate for change, we built a coalition of advocates from the governor to the supervisors to the League of Women Voters, all intent upon making our election system better. It was inclusive and involved communication at every level.

> "Your credibility is essential to effecting change."

Change can be unsettling. It takes us out of our comfort zone. When I was mayor and someone would describe himself as enamored with change, thriving on change, a change agent, I would think to myself, "not likely." The straightforward leader needs to keep in mind the tendency of people to resist change at every turn. In an unpredictable world of transformation, most people try to maintain constants through relationships and daily habits. Managing change in the workforce means taking people from what's familiar to an unknown place. The leader makes change comfortable by removing uncertainty and helping those involved see it as a step to a better and more secure future.

"In eight years as mayor, Pam Iorio changed the professional culture of the city's bureaucracy."

St. Petersburg Times, March 27, 2011

It was time for change at the City of Tampa, a large bureaucracy with approximately 4,500 employees. Like many organizations it was steeped in tradition and fixed in its ways. I arrived at City Hall in 2003 with a specific agenda for change that was understood and expected by the public. I had campaigned on this agenda and presented it at dozens of campaign forums. I knew it was the right direction for the city.

Large organizations and industries are slow to change. Look at the automobile industry and its financial problems. Government intervention was required to avoid the collapse of some of our nation's best-known brands. The industry was sluggish in adapting to new realities and it almost caused their demise. Government has those same tendencies. Many employees don't understand the need for change and their leaders have never properly articulated the requirement for a different mission or structure. Getting employees to view their jobs in a different light demands proper guidance and leadership, or it can lead to unhappiness and discontent. Here, too, communication from the top plays such an important role.

Directing change in a world where change has changed is analogous to climbing a mountain that has no summit. The climb is never ending. In the past you may have encountered a plateau. You hiked along the ridge at a leisurely pace before starting to ascend again. In our new world of change, the climb is always upward, there is no flat terrain. The never-ceasing goal is constant progress. There is no peak because the new norm keeps raising the pinnacle ever higher. *Celebrate and acknowledge success along the way, but never stop the climb.* This is the 21st Century version of directing change. This concept may be uncomfortable to those who want the plateau, the flat terrain. The leader has to show how the constant ascent leads to a better place for the organization and the employee.

Just because you as the leader recognize that change has changed doesn't mean your employees see it that way or, if they do, agree that it is good. At my neighborhood grocery store I chatted with the cashier who lamented the rapid changes occurring at her store. No sooner had she learned the latest in scanning and paperless technology, than she had to learn something new. I could tell this was stressful for her. It can be unsettling to know we always have to learn something different. An employee may be concerned about their capacity to grasp the latest technology, or that it will make them less valuable to the organization. These are valid concerns that a leader cannot ignore and should address through constant communication.

In my eight years running the City of Tampa I directed change driven by two radically different sets of circumstances.

The first: Four years of initiatives, investments, new ideas, and a fresh organization.

The second: Four years of strategic contraction, declining revenues, and internal reorganization.

What did these two change experiences have in common? They required long-term thinking, a sense of mission, the involvement of employees at all levels, constant communication, an emphasis on results, and strategic planning. Each approach recognizes that change has changed; the status quo is not an option.

Any leader will tell you that it is a lot more exciting to implement the first course than the second. With a vibrant economy, increasing housing values, optimism, and expansion, it is easy to lead in times of abundance. The second way is the more difficult one and involves tough decisions. Ultimately, it is rewarding to see a restructured organization that accomplishes its mission with less. As a leader, you are called upon to lead in all circumstances. Straightforward leaders are vital in the tough times. The qualities and competencies they have developed are essential for directing change.

As a new mayor embarking on my change journey, I assembled a quality team and focused on our vision, mission, and strategic goals. Our vision:

Tampa will be recognized as a diverse, progressive city; it will be celebrated as the most desirable place to live, learn, work, and play.

Our mission involved a commitment to excellence that supported the vision:

The City of Tampa's mission is to deliver outstanding services to enhance the quality of life of our community.

These statements may seem simple, but they focused the staff and were powerful recruitment tools. Top quality people want to belong to an organization with a sense of purpose. People want to be proud of where they work and that they are participating in something with a larger, overarching purpose. There are thousands of government entities in this country; people of excellence gravitate towards those not content with the status quo. They want to see a purpose, a plan, and achievable goals.

"The mission animates the entire organization."

Strategic goals provided the outline we followed during my eight year tenure. Strategic goals are the framework—allowing individuals at many different levels of an organization to clearly identify how they fit into the overall plan and how to allocate resources. If your organization doesn't have clearly defined strategic goals, your effectiveness is greatly diminished. *Everyone in the organization must have a sense of purpose.*

If you serve on a board of directors for a business or non-profit entity, ask the CEO to articulate the group's vision and mission; then review the strategic plan and goals. Without such planning, your organization has a problem. If they exist, your next step is to determine if the goals are integrated into the budget process, the priorities of the staff, and what the top leader communicates internally and externally. If they are not integrated, there is still a problem because in all likelihood the organization is lurching from one idea and project to another, absent a cohesive framework for change and progress. Without a clear plan, your organization is not only wasting valuable time and money, but it can't possibly direct change in a meaningful way and position itself for the future.

"Strategy provides a sense of purpose."

Establishing priorities is critical. You don't waste time and resources on other distracting activities. You can imagine the number of people trying to pull a mayor in many directions. Constituents, community and business leaders, employees and supporters all see you as the means to getting *their* priorities accomplished. Where a leadership vacuum exists, others will fill the void. Running an organization, or managing your personal life, requires adherence to your goals—not someone else's. It is the achievement of your goals that defines your success.

When I was mayor, our six strategic goals were to:

- Invest in Tampa's neighborhoods
- Be a city of the arts
- Create a downtown residential community
- Achieve economic development in our most challenged areas—using East Tampa as a model
- Be an efficient city government focused on customer service
- Make regional mass transit a reality

These six goals became the focal point of my eight years in office. They were reinforced in printed materials and on our website, and were mentioned in virtually every speech I made. For your goals to be real to your employees and customers repetition is necessary—we spent considerable time in our first year meeting with different levels of city staff to ensure the goals were clearly understood and the objectives for each department were established. The staff was involved in setting objectives and timelines, making sure that they were realistic and achievable. An open dialogue was encouraged to learn what obstacles departments faced in achieving progress. These discussions laid the groundwork for the budget process so we could allocate resources specifically directed at meeting our goals.

What struck me when I became mayor was the absence of accountability standards expected from the top management. If someone was not doing a good job, even if it was glaringly obvious to the organization and to the community, it didn't seem to matter. That changed right away. The objectives we set to support the strategic goals meant that top management would be held responsible and accountable for achieving success. *Without a system of accountability you can't seriously pursue change.*

You may already have a high-functioning team or you may need to infuse the organization with new, fresh talent. As a new leader, don't be too quick to cast off existing staff unless you have a compelling reason to do so. Just because current staff hasn't thrived under the old regime does not mean they can't when guided by a straightforward leader. Motivating and getting the best from the people who have been with the organization for a long time is important, not only because they have institutional knowledge and capabilities, but because they tend to have the strongest ties to people further down the organizational chart—the grassroots implementers of change. It is critical, however, that longtime staff truly believes in the change taking place, not just paying lip service to it, while in fact holding fast to the old ways. *There must be congruency between actions and words.* At every level of the organization your staff must be loyal to the mission.

"Hiring the right people is critical for change."

98

Directing change often means bringing new people into the organization. You may need a particular expertise that members of the present team lack. Also, despite your best efforts, not all existing staff may embrace a fresh calling, direction, and style. You and your top staff must be on the same wavelength. It took me two full years to put my team in place. It is not easy to recruit the best people; in government you can't always pay the highest salary and there are no stock options. That's where the sense of purpose comes in. When I hired administrators and department heads, I talked about how we could and would make a difference to the City of Tampa, thus leaving a legacy of a better community. The challenge of doing that was more important than money to the fine team we brought together.

Communicating the strategic goals, which is the engine for continuous change and improvement, is a daily process. Employees should know their role, your shareholders must understand your strategy, the media and all stakeholder groups (including taxpayers if you are in government) have to see the vision and understand the plan. Again, communication at all levels is a key competency for the straightforward leader.

The best example during my term in office of taking the vision, mission, and strategic goals to heart and producing tremendous results can be seen in our police department and the unprecedented 61.5 percent drop in crime the city experienced. I credit both of the police chiefs I served with for their straightforward leadership which led to the successful implementation of major change.

When I first took office, Tampa had one of the highest crime rates for a city of its size. This was a serious problem and it needed to be addressed through a focused effort. I shared my goal to dramatically reduce crime with my newly appointed Chief of Police, Stephen Hogue. He accepted responsibility for the mission and developed a strategy. He reorganized the department, and held officers accountable for the decrease in crime within their districts. A program was developed that focused on the four types of crime most likely to affect our citizens; the ones that could lead to even worse offenses. The results were astonishing and steady. By the end of my eight years, crime in Tampa had declined by 61.5 percent, far greater than that of surrounding counties or the State of Florida. We are now among the safest cities of our size.

Chief Hogue and his successor, Jane Castor, adhered to all of the elements of a straightforward leader in directing change. They embraced the vision and mission and developed a strategy. They made sure that the right people were in place, and that they believed in the mission and were motivated to carry out the plan at all levels. The message was communicated every single day; community involvement was solicited and obtained. Employees at all levels were engaged and methods were adjusted based upon their suggestions for improvement. The continual decline in the crime rate was celebrated and our police officers received many accolades for their hard work and commitment. The amount of change that occurred within the Tampa Police Department in an eight-year time frame was unprecedented, yet it was embraced because it produced positive results that the officers could see for themselves. Everyone wants to be proud of where they work, and our police officers had every right to be proud of their work to make Tampa a safer, more livable city.

As you guide change it is critical to celebrate accomplishments along the way. The ascent up the mountain is ongoing and you need to recognize the milestones. We instituted a yearly "State of the City" event where we recapped the accomplishments of the previous year. It gave me an opportunity to laud the work of the city's employees and recognize their accomplishments.

Sometimes dramatic, unanticipated events will alter your strategies. Had we been hit by a hurricane during my tenure, which was probable given our location, our strategic focus would have shifted. As things happened, we were hit by a storm of another sort—the "Great Recession." This caused us to shift priorities and focus our energies

"Stick to the plan."

100

and ideas on the task of shrinking city government. Since one of our initial goals was to make city government more efficient, that became a focal point of our effort.

The Great Recession caused hardship for millions of people as well as organizations of all types throughout the United States. Businesses, non-profits, and government at all levels had to scale back their operations. Many businesses had to close their doors. Unemployment soared. Tampa's revenues, like those of all local governments, dropped precipitously.

New circumstances meant a new plan. We had to internally reorganize our large bureaucracy, beyond what we had done in our first four years. The goal was to protect services while cutting and consolidating. Unlike downturns of the past that were temporary and could be addressed with short-term strategies, this economic downturn was predicted to last for many years. The changes we made had to reflect a longer horizon to meet the challenge.

At the same time, another of our goals had been to bolster the city's financial reserves and set aside money for emergencies. Early in my tenure, the city's external financial auditors cautioned us that our reserves were too low. Like a corporation, a city relies on having a substantial cash reserve to provide financial stability and a cushion for emergencies. As a city that is vulnerable to hurricanes, we have to set aside substantial reserves in case a major storm hits. We had set a goal during my first term, which coincided with robust economic growth, to build our reserves from $50 million to approximately $120 million. When the recession hit during my second term, it was tempting to stop adding to the reserves. Some asked why we should cut positions and reduce services when reserves were available and could be tapped. In my view, that approach would have been both short-sighted given the long-term nature of the problem and counterproductive to the long-term health of our city.

For these reasons, during this recession we determined we had to achieve two goals: strategically shrink city government and build up our rainy-day reserves. Both would lead to greater stability and sustainability.

Every organization has its own way of downsizing when faced with an economic crisis. It depends on the product you produce and deliver, whether the decline is short-term or long-term, and how your reductions affect productivity and the customer. In government, our customer is the taxpayer. Our product is the myriad services, ranging from potable and reclaimed water, wastewater treatment, garbage collection, parks and recreation, to public safety and a great deal more in between.

Our reduction goals were two-fold. One, do the right thing for the customer. Consider how any cut will affect them. Two, no whining, complaining, or hand-wringing. It would reflect poorly on the entire organization. Plenty of people were suffering in the community and we were not going to be seen as complainers. Operating from a realistic perspective, knowing that change has changed, there is no room for self-pity.

Ultimately, over four years, we cut $124 million from the budget, trimmed the workforce by 672 positions through attrition and layoffs, stabilized personnel costs by reducing pay increases, and tripled our financial reserves from $50 million to $150 million, in excess of the goal we had set years earlier.

This success was made possible by the involvement of employees at many different levels of city government. Through an employee-based suggestion program called the Efficiency and Effectiveness Task Force, employees worked in teams and ideas came from all levels on ways to save money. The best ideas usually come from the people who actually did the work, and over four years these employee teams and their suggestions saved the city $16 million. Their direct involvement also helped employees understand the financial difficulties the city faced and the solutions needed to deal with the changing circumstances.

This four-year process and our success in meeting our change goals taught me two important lessons about large organizations. First, *there is room to trim in most large organizations*. If you look carefully at each of your functions, you can find new and better ways to do business. It may cause discontent at first, and it's not easy, but there are always ways to improve. No organization can afford to remain static.

Second, *smaller is sometimes better*. Departments shrunk dramatically, yet we were still able to deliver the important services. We eliminated layers of management and our organization improved. Too many people were in supervisory roles that didn't translate to added value for the team. In the end, we built a leaner and stronger city government.

Proof of how shrinking can actually improve efficiency came after Police Chief Hogue eliminated an *entire* administrative division within his department. "The department runs much more efficiently," he told me after the changes had been in effect for some time. "We get more work done, faster." And, of course, we saved the taxpayers hundreds of thousands of dollars.

"Smaller can spark efficiencies."

I continually took the pulse of our top managers to ensure cuts were being made with the over-arching concept of change in mind. Change does not mean taking the same deck of cards and reshuffling them; it means removing some cards from the deck altogether and bringing in new cards. In a change environment you have to caution your team to spend more time thinking about new ways to do business rather than defending against reductions. With only so many hours and so much energy in a day, the focus needs to be on a different way of operating.

The stark reduction in revenues made it imperative, and, in some ways, easier to transform the organization. In my first term I met resistance from within the city as new initiatives and new hires changed the culture of the bureaucracy. A changing climate was difficult for some employees to absorb, despite my efforts to communicate with them and enlist their involvement. When fiscal realities made change a necessity in my second term, it was less about the environment than about the bottom line. Employees could better understand that dynamic. With my executive team firmly established during the first four years, we could address the problem in a unified and cohesive manner.

Because change has changed, today's leader must effectively guide the team on that never-ending ascent up the mountain. The inner leadership traits of honesty and humility, kindness and respect, measured and thoughtful decision-making, a resilient spirit, all contribute to the straightforward leader's positive and reinforcing personal interactions that bring about change. The best outcome is when people understand change has changed and feel good about the future. The straightforward leader casts change as a better way for the organization to grow and thrive.

Choose Your Change Battles

Though change has changed, you can't win all of your change battles. Prioritize the ones that matter the most and save the rest for another day when you have had time to build consensus. As with most things, timing is important.

In politics I see newly elected officials rush headlong into fulfilling campaign promises, often alienating people with other points of view. These are the times in which we live, when checking off a list of so called "accomplishments" and pleasing one segment of the political spectrum is more important than effective long-term change that is inclusive and respectful of all sides. I have witnessed this across the country with issues of school reform and retirement benefit restructuring. There is no doubt that both areas need a 21st Century update. Change has changed, and old templates may require a new approach. However, the executive who forces through change that leaves employees, customers, or constituents feeling powerless is making a mistake. It is a short-term victory.

The straightforward leader takes the time to work with those whose lives will be affected by the change, whatever it may be. In the City of Tampa, once I explained our financial situation to our employees and the limited options we had, they understood that the pay increases they previously received would not be possible in the foreseeable future. It was an economic reality. Treat people with respect and bring them into the conversation, particularly when it affects their career paths and their plans for retirement.

When choosing your change battles, applying that important straightforward leadership characteristic—the careful use of power—is essential. When given a top position, CEO, governor, or mayor, your style of wielding power is central to your long-term effectiveness in producing real change. It's easy for a person in a position of power to impose their will in an autocratic manner. The real leadership talent is restructuring and rearranging without the ham-fisted use of power. Many politicians like to describe themselves as strong leaders when they have gotten their way on an issue by bulldozing through the opposition. That's not straightforward leadership. That's just the imprudent use of power. The raw use of power in our political system today has led to a polarization of our political institutions and, to some extent, our society. People don't see politicians as consensus builders; instead they view them as clear winners and losers in an ongoing battle. Real leadership starts with a vision, a buy-in from your employees, and, ultimately, your customers or constituents.

Once you have articulated the vision, mission, and goals, you set a course of change that involves a number of decisions. Not all change is equal. In the City of Tampa, changing the professional culture by bringing in leaders with different perspectives was of utmost importance. Our strategic goals prioritized what was central, and that's what we worked on first. Other changes had to wait.

It is human nature to want things to stay as they were.

At the start of my second term in 2007, it was clear that the City of Tampa needed serious restructuring. The state legislature had taken action that adversely impacted the revenues of all local governments. With revenues down and the economic downturn continuing into the foreseeable future, we needed to streamline and consolidate. We either took control of change or it would dictate to us.

"Even your own handpicked team can be resistant to change."

Our chief of staff proposed a consolidation of a variety of internal functions. Over the years, city departments had become too decentralized. Although information technology (IT), fiscal, and personnel were all separate, centralized departments, many agencies still had their own IT, budget, and human resources staffers. This gave departments a sense that they had more control over their own productivity, but from an overall broader organizational perspective, it wasn't efficient. By transferring these staff into the larger, centralized departments, we could cross-train, utilize their skills for the entire city, not just one department, and achieve efficiencies. I had put this change battle off during my first term. It was not a priority compared to everything else we wanted to get done, but in my second term cost savings were a necessity and by then I had the right people in place to ensure a smooth transition.

To my surprise, aside from my chief of staff, none of my top administrators wanted this change. All argued against it. You would have thought that this idea was being presented to a group of entrenched city government personnel. Yet, these were all people I had appointed and had been with the city only as long as I had.

Why would a group of managers I had hired to lead change resist it? All my administrators and direct reports were people of the highest caliber. Well educated and experienced, they were bringing much-needed change to the organization. Yet, in this case they were uniformly resistant to change. Did they really think the new direction was wrong? After consideration, I decided that was not the case; I saw another dynamic at work. When your staff knows they are held accountable for progress, they are afraid to lose control over parts of the organization within their purview. Paradoxically, this good thing—accountability—can make leaders more resistant to another good thing—necessary change. The more successful you are in your job, the less likely you want to change the current structure. That structure was partially responsible for the success you achieved. Why would you want to change it?

After listening to my staff, I found the root of the problem was their collective lack of faith that the centralized approach would serve their individual departments as well as the decentralized approach had. Centralized to them meant more bureaucracy, less responsiveness. They were concerned. What if the new, consolidated IT department was not responsive to them? What if they couldn't get their priorities addressed quickly and they lost, rather than gained, efficiencies?

Other problems soon became apparent. The budget analyst in the Parks and Recreation department might have also become the "go-to" person for other departmental matters. The distinction between the job description and the reality of the work they performed had blurred and the administrator didn't want to give up the productivity of the employee who performed multiple tasks that could not be gleaned from a table of organization.

Regardless of these arguments, the chief of staff and I were confident that the outcome of consolidation would be not only a savings of money but a more efficient city government. We knew that at the helm of each of the departments into which staff would be consolidated were good, capable leaders, who were committed to making the transition work.

As you choose your change battles, don't give up on a course of action simply because you encounter opposition. It will likely be the initial reaction in most instances. Work through it, spend time understanding the root of the opposition. The disruption that is caused in the short-term can be ameliorated through long-term benefits that will become apparent as the change takes hold.

In this case, the discussion about consolidation went on for months as I privately met with each administrator to explore their concerns. The longer we waited, the longer it was going to take to realize the budget savings. Finally, while I respected all of their good arguments against the consolidations, I directed that the plan move forward. Given our team's track record in managing change, I believed this new approach was achievable. To their credit, not a single administrator uttered a word of discontent from that day forward. Over the years we had become one team, built upon mutual trust and respect. Once a decision was made, no one complained, they moved on to implement it. The consolidations took place and saved the city millions. Further, we have a better-trained and more flexible workforce. This was an issue where, as mayor, I could make the final decision and move the organization forward on my say so.

You can't win all your change battles. I lost one where the decision was not mine alone because I couldn't convince the city council of the need for change. That plan was to privatize the city's janitorial and security services. We already had a hybrid system with city employees as well as some private janitorial companies and private security companies working for the city. Most governments had already gone the privatization route a long time ago, so it was hardly an original idea.

We also wanted to privatize warehouse operations that held inventory for our utility systems such as water and wastewater. These efforts would have saved several millions of dollars and our service level to the taxpayer would not have been affected.

Based upon the merits of the proposal it should have sailed through, but just because an idea is logical and a money saver doesn't mean it's going to happen.

The Tampa City Council would not approve the plan. They were concerned that existing employees would lose their jobs when we contracted with a private firm That is part of the give and take of any large, complex organization. Other factors are bound to weigh in on a decision. Councils and boards think differently than CEOs. In this case, once employees went directly to council with concerns about job loss, I knew this was one change that wasn't going to happen.

Choose your change battles. Logic and the promise of efficiencies don't always win the day. We didn't bring the privatization plan up again even though the city continued to absorb revenue losses and to endure employee layoffs in other areas. Trying to push it through would have adversely affected my relations with council, which would have negatively affected the city as a whole. Each attempt at change needs to be looked at independently; the pros and cons evaluated in the context of your strategic goals and larger vision.

Change takes time. The major museum and park project in our downtown core, took many twists and turns during its development. We were building a new art museum, a beautiful new waterfront park, laying the underground infrastructure for a new children's museum, building a segment of the Tampa Riverwalk, repairing a seawall, and rebuilding an urban park adjacent to an office tower. Construction was complex and a lot had to be demolished before new construction started. During construction, regular tours were scheduled with reporters and others in the community to help them visualize the beauty of the end product. That isn't easy when you are standing in a mud hole. Sharing the vision is an ongoing process and is important even after a new project or product line is launched.

"Revolutionary change takes evolutionary time."

Tampa Tribune columnist Steve Otto looked at me dubiously as I waxed enthusiastic about the new Curtis Hixon Waterfront Park and museums. "Did you say 'transformative?'" he joked as dust and dirt blew in our faces as we toured the site in a golf cart. Patience paid off and while many were unconvinced during the construction, the end result was stunning and a truly remarkable addition to our downtown.

Positive results make the pain of change worth the work. Directing change is a major responsibility of a leader but choosing your battles makes your work easier. Your strategic goals help you frame priorities and decide which elements of change need to be addressed first. If the change is complex and involves a fundamental redirection of the way business is done, involve your employees and stakeholders in the process. Be inclusive. Use your power carefully, recognize that not all change can occur at once, and bring your employees and customers along on the journey if you want lasting progress.

Embrace Technological Advances

Our future and our competitive edge depend on technology. Whether in the private, public, or nonprofit sector, today's leaders must grasp these new and ever changing concepts, principles, and applications to stay ahead of the game. Technology goes beyond the merely technical; leaders must embrace these new tools and apply them to all aspects of their business. Not doing so can have unintended consequences as it did in the 2000 presidential election. Had the supervisors of elections and the state division of elections kept pace with technology, the fiasco of 2000 might never have occurred. At the time, most counties in Florida used punch card technology dating back to the 1970s. It had never been a problem because elections were never this close, but in 2000 this old technology affected ballot design and made it hard in some cases to determine a voter's intent and that affected how ballots were counted. Here we were, a great world power with a political system held out as the gold standard for others, yet the mechanics of tabulating votes in Florida were archaic.

Today, you simply cannot afford to stand still for even one week when it comes to technological change. *Change has changed, and technology is at the core of this new 21st Century model.*

Establish your technological knowledge and credentials, if you choose to be a leader. As someone who grew up pre-digital, I have had to make a deliberate and conscious effort to learn the new social media and all of its applications. Like many, at first I resisted it, but having seen the tremendous benefits from community outreach and research to coalition building and innovation, I'm a convert.

This effort is analogous to the initiative you must employ to further develop your inner leadership qualities. Just as it takes mental discipline to admit mistakes and accept responsibility, or easily to forgive others so, too, it takes a concerted effort to learn and welcome change.

More than the generations that have come before, today's youth have grown up with technology and consequently their brains are wired differently. The use of technology has been shown to alter the way we think. Consider the extraordinary group of young leaders like Facebook's Mark Zuckerberg, Twitter's Chairman Jack Dorsey, YouTube co-founder & CEO Chad Hurley and Skype co-founder Niklas Zennstrom who have taken cutting edge technical ideas and turned them into multi-million, even multi-billion dollar enterprises in a relatively short period of time. Their edge and expertise come from growing up in a wired world.

The use of technology is not an option for today's leaders. It is a required competency.

As a leader, you may look no further than our young people to see the path to the future. I often observe the consumer habits of our two children, in their early twenties, as a bellwether. Newspapers are an obvious example. Both have grown up in a household where two newspapers were delivered daily, where both parents religiously read and commented on the stories, and where their mother frequently highlighted items of interest. Yet neither reads a printed newspaper. Both receive all of their news on-line. When I point out an article that I want one of them to read, the response is, "send me the link."

It doesn't take a focus group to tell you that the print newspaper as we know it is not in our future.

Social media is no different than the invention of the telephone which fundamentally changed the way we communicated with one another. At first it was unfamiliar, but soon society and business could not function without it. Managed properly, social media improves the flow of information and provides a platform for open dialogue. It offers many new efficiencies from which leaders and stakeholders can benefit. Today's businesses are finding different ways to communicate with customers, and with social media, you can get instant feedback on your product or service. You can connect with ambassadors for your cause, potential customers, and investors, and gain valuable insight from your market.

As a leader, you can't be a dinosaur and you better make sure you don't have dinosaurs in your organization. IT is no longer a support function that receives little attention; it is now central to your organization's advancement. The interest in and support of technology must start at the top and have strong leaders driving it forward.

The IT person who has served the organization well for many years may not serve it well in the future if he hasn't kept up. Does your IT person know that change has changed? Is there a reluctance to embrace the newest systems and applications? Most important, does your IT person *think* in new and different ways? These are important questions for leaders to probe. If your IT person isn't on the cutting edge, your organization won't be either. One executive shared that people in his firm weren't sure what to do with Facebook. This seemed odd since their company produced a consumer-based product, and it seemed obvious that Facebook could play a role in their marketing efforts. The explanation for this disconnect soon became clear; the executive responsible for technology didn't understand Facebook and therefore did not know how it could be applied to their business. He viewed Facebook simply as a social phenomenon, a fad, with no value to the business.

Regardless of where you started on the technological spectrum, you must end up in the thick of what's new and different. For any large organization this means continual investment to keep internal technology up-to-date and to learn about how to use what's available outside. It also means hiring the brightest minds in the field.

The Path to Straightforward Leadership—Step 4: Knowing that Change Has Changed

The straightforward leader can direct change in a meaningful and lasting way by:

- Understanding that change has changed; it is rapid and never ending
- Methodically developing your vision, mission, and strategic goals
- Bringing people along on the change journey
- Understanding that your actions and style, not your title, qualify you as a leader
- Choosing your change battles by setting priorities through your strategic goals and acting once you have heard all sides
- Staying abreast of technological advancements and incorporating them quickly into your organization

The straightforward leader understands there's no going back. The exponential rate of change is a new reality. He believes and communicates that change is not to be feared, while knowing that most do fear it. Change represents a way to do the job better. It is an opportunity to find new ways for an organization to grow and prosper. The leader, regardless of the mandate for change, must do it in a way that brings the rest of the team along. Strategic thinking leads to long-term results and that is the ultimate goal of any change.

Chapter Five

———

LIVE A CENTERED LIFE

OUNDING FATHER BENJAMIN FRANKLIN IS the quintessential
example of a centered life. At the time of his death at the
age of 84, Franklin had amassed a lifetime of achievements
which would be virtually unheard of today. Diplomat, author, scientist, politician, businessman, philanthropist, Franklin embodied the
best qualities of leadership. One would think that with all of these
achievements, Franklin would be content, but that wasn't Franklin's
nature. He understood that in addition to his professional achievements, he had to work on developing what we, today, would call a
"centered" inner life. In his typically organized fashion, he compiled a list of "Thirteen Virtues" that he studied regularly to improve
himself. It is said that when he completed the list he would go back
to the first and start over. These virtues ranged from "Order." *Let all
your things have their places; let each part of your business have its
time,* to "Moderation," *Avoid extremes, forbear resenting injuries so
much as you think they deserve.* Not exactly catchy homilies by today's standards, but the important point is that Franklin understood

the importance of working to make yourself a better person and that is very relevant to today's leaders.

Franklin's disciplined approach to his own de-
velopment undoubtedly helped him succeed in other areas. A successful leader strives to build a balanced life — not perfect, but centered. We are a title-driven society and many people feel they are not successful if they don't have an important position in the work-force, don't make a lot of money or wield power and influence. Those things don't measure your contribution to society. It is a mistake for us to see leadership only in the context of the workforce, a limitation that fails to appreciate the many skills and competencies of people from all walks of life. Earlier, I quoted President John Quincy Adams' inspiring words: *If your actions inspire others to dream more, learn more, do more and become more, you are a leader.* Leadership is the act of guiding others to improve. That's easy to see in the context of a formal organization where achievements are noted. It is a little harder to recognize outside of the workplace, but I frequently witness it from all spectrums of our society, and I want those who exhibit this straightforward leadership to see it in themselves.

> "You have to lead yourself well before you can lead others."

Living a centered life is central to being a leader. A friend will not come to you for advice and guidance if your own life is not one of balance and moderation. Leading your family means you have developed habits and traits that cause your children or others to consider you a role model. A centered life means you can be relied upon to tackle the difficult because you have shown the discipline and strength to handle adversity. In this chapter, we will explore those qualities and practices.

Living a centered life is congruent with the straightforward leader in the professional setting as well. For this reason, it is important to pay as much attention to your personal life as you do your professional. People in the workforce want to see a leader who exhibits the same characteristics in and out of the workplace. Your personal values and your professional actions should be in harmony. Leading yourself is the basis for leading others.

In the first chapter we discussed the importance of being honest with yourself so that you can readily accept your shortfalls at the same time as you work to improve them and continually seek to develop your inner leadership qualities. All of those qualities, honesty and humility, a positive and optimistic outlook, a measured and thoughtful demeanor, the ability to admit mistakes and accept responsibility, the ability to compete without making excuses, resiliency, respect for others, and the careful exercise of power—require constant work and discipline. That same dynamic is required for the development of your personal side. To live a centered life we come full circle, embracing not only those inner leadership qualities, but the essential habits and practices that define you as an individual.

Our discussion of personal attributes in this chapter is neither all inclusive nor definitive. There are innumerable books dedicated to the myriad ways we can be better people. The particular set of traits and habits I describe comes from winnowing down what I have learned from observing straightforward leaders. It is rare to find one person who exhibits all of these traits, all of the time. The important point is that you recognize the need to make these habits part of your daily life. Developing these essential practices is a work in progress. Remember, when Franklin finished his list of thirteen virtues, he went back to the beginning and started over.

In my view, you have achieved a centered life when:

- *You are focused, well-rounded and caring*: You deal with personal setbacks and problems in a realistic way, charting a positive path forward. You set goals, take care of your body and mind, protect your privacy, and treat everyone as you would like to be treated.

- *You believe in yourself and have the confidence to try new things:* You are able to take risks because you understand your capabilities and are not afraid to try something new.
- *You create harmony between your home life and work:* Your home life and your work life are in a happy equilibrium that allows you to feel good about what you are able to accomplish each day.

Focused, Well-Rounded, and Caring

Former Tampa Bay Buccaneer and Indianapolis Colts Coach Tony Dungy is quite possibly the best example of an individual who has a totally integrated professional and personal life. His first book, *Quiet Strength*[8], is a must read for lessons in leadership. Dungy is a man of deep religious faith and it guides his life. He embraces every attribute of the straightforward leader. I hold him out as a role model because he embodies the qualities of a focused, well-rounded, and caring individual who lives a centered life. He finds a way to see a positive direction regardless of the setback or tragedy. His daily life, his habits and practices, lead others to look to him for guidance and advice.

In his book, Dungy describes the emotions he experienced cleaning out his office at One Buc Place, after being fired as the head coach of the Buccaneers. In six seasons he had built a team around values and character, made the play-offs three times, and had the best winning record of any coach in Buccaneer history. He was revered by the community. Yet, there he was on a rainy night in January 2002 cleaning out his office, a solitary figure carrying the boxes to his SUV. Filled with doubt and uncertainty about the

---

8. Tony Dungy, *Quiet Strength: the Principles, Practices, & Priorities of a Winning Life*, Illinois: Tyndale House Publishers, Inc., 2007.

future? Of course, Dungy, like all of us when faced with a setback, wondered what his future would hold. He described his thoughts during his drive home:

> *I kept reminding myself that I would move on, that things would turn out all right professionally, that Lauren and the children were resilient enough to handle all of this.*

Tony and his wife Lauren are individuals of strong character. Complaining and dwelling on the firing was simply not in their makeup. Both handle adversity with grace and dignity. Disappointment, yes, but no bitterness or finger-pointing. Simply an acceptance of reality and, most important, a belief in finding a way forward.

Dungy immediately started thinking about how he could become even more involved in the meaningful youth charities he was already a part of in Tampa. His first thought was about how he could give more to others. Then a phone call from the owner of the Indianapolis Colts provided a new opportunity for the coach. The rest of the story: the Colts won the Super Bowl under Dungy's leadership. Having reached the pinnacle of his professional career, he retired from coaching. Today he contributes through his books, speeches, and charitable work. He is rightly widely admired as an outstanding leader in our country.

Tony Dungy's approach to his career setback illustrates the best of the straightforward leader: an ability to see adversity as opportunity. He describes the ultimately positive impact his firing had on him:

> "Squarely face your problems."

> *But I think my getting fired had an even greater impact. It's easy to be gracious when you're getting carried off the field in celebration. It's more difficult when you're asked to pack up your desk and your pass code doesn't work anymore. I think people look*

more closely at our actions in the rough times, when the emotions are raw and our guard is down. That's when our true character shows and we find out if our faith is real.

Dungy turned the negative experience positive. He saw it as a growing moment, a time when he had to dig deep and find inner strength. When adversity struck, the alignment of his personal and professional values and qualities demonstrated the strength that comes from a centered life.

Not all problems have a solution; some you carry with you all of your life. A centered life is not necessarily about resolving an issue, it is about coming to grips with the reality of your situation and finding a way forward. I know people who have severe health issues or their family members do. Those health issues are not going away, and will worsen. What has gone away is the feeling of helplessness. They face the reality of their circumstance, and chart a course of action that moves their family forward.

I will never forget an encounter I had with a mother at an autism charity walk. As I greeted the participants, she shared her story with me. Her fourteen-year-old son was severely autistic and she worked full-time as a nurse. She said something I would never have expected: "My son has been the greatest blessing in our lives. I have learned so much and am a better person because of him." I was overwhelmed not only by what she said, but by the sincere, direct way she delivered this powerful message to me. I was witness to a leader, a person who, through difficulty, found a positive way to direct herself and her family.

When you are a leader, or if you aspire to be one, people will look at how you tackle your personal problems as a way to measure your ability to do the same at work. The straightforward leader finds the way forward even under the worst possible circumstance. They take the next step, do the next thing, to manage and direct their life.

In your professional life, if a leadership void exists, someone will fill it. The same is true in your personal life. If you are aimless, without a clear path for your future, someone will come along and direct your life for you. It may not be where you want to go, but in the absence of setting your own direction, it's where you will end up. Leaders direct their personal lives. Though the course of life has many unpredictable turns, an overall direction is needed to live a centered life.

At the heart of a straightforward leader is a person who wants to leave his mark on the world, and, in doing so, make it a little bit better than how he found it. The organization he leads keeps getting stronger, making a superior product or delivering the best service. Its impact is meant to be lasting. So, too, in the personal lives of these leaders, I see goals and aspirations that have a greater meaning.

As mayor, I met a large number of citizens who were doers, real go-getters in the community. They took it upon themselves to try to fix the various ills in society through their charitable work. They ranged across the spectrum—those with high-level corporate positions to those with no professional position at all. From the bank executive to the Little League coach, they sought to make a difference through their contributions to the community.

Each had a clear direction for his life, a personal mission statement that defined the way they lived and led. Events may change the timing or the exact course of their lives, but the overall goals remain. In all cases, they defined success not in terms of what it did for them, but what it did for others.

The importance of having a vision, mission, goals, and strategy for your business or organization is obvious. While you may not formalize these elements in your personal life, merely thinking in these terms helps you focus on the long-term. Some people I know do write down their personal strategic plan and review it periodically. Others mentally keep track. It is helpful to articulate your plans to the person to whom you are closest, such as your spouse or partner, so that your lives move together towards results that you both agree upon.

Believing in something bigger than your own needs and desires means you consider those of others. You can't be a leader if your world is insular, where you occupy front and center at all times. The leader helps people in ways large and small, from their family, to their friends, to their spiritual home, to charitable organizations, to the neighborhood. This broader outreach means you are putting others first, helping them grow and change, just as you do in your professional life. The personal and professional become one, and both identify you as a leader.

A healthy lifestyle is another important part of a centered life. This involves daily habits that keep you performing at your best. As a leader you want your organization to be healthy, vibrant, and energetic. Shouldn't that also be part of your personal image? Taking care of yourself physically affects your mental state, and both warrant your attention as a leader.

When I started my professional career, I was in my twenties, and I didn't give much thought to exercise or nutrition. Like most young people I didn't see the need. I ate fast food and didn't have an organized exercise program.

In 1997, I joined Leadership Florida, a statewide organization of business and political leaders who seek to make the state of Florida a better place. I was amazed by how many of the state's top CEOs built their day around exercise. Of the 50 people in our group at least two-thirds were exercise buffs. We even changed our morning start time because so many liked to run or exercise in the gym to start the day. At that time I was the mother of a seven- and a nine-year-old, as well as the Supervisor of Elections. My idea of exercise was riding my bike in the neighborhood with the kids.

When I became mayor, its challenging schedule forced me to think differently about exercise. I better understood its benefits and place in my life. Then, as my father's health declined, I began to experience physical problems. My doctor told me what I needed most was exercise to alleviate stress. He was right. I learned a valuable lesson about taking care of myself first so I could live a better life and be able to help those around me.

Finding time for yourself is always a challenge. There are many competing demands on your time. It's not easy and usually requires some sacrifice or at least a re-ordering of your priorities. I rearranged my work schedule so that my very early morning hours from 6:00 a.m. to 7:00 a.m. were spent at the gym. It meant I couldn't attend early breakfast meetings, but that was a small price to pay for getting my exercise in before the start of my official duties. I had to change the way I thought. Exercise needs to be scheduled and to become a habit. It cannot be optional, because optional means you won't do it. Think of your core daily habits and then think about stopping any one of them. You wouldn't. They are habits for a reason—they help you live your life the way you think it needs to be lived.

Earlier I discussed the importance of giving yourself time to think, particularly when you have important decisions to make. My new exercise habit gave me the opportunity to do both—take care of myself physically, and think through issues and problems. I have arrived at more solutions to issues in the gym than anywhere else.

As a leader, it's easy to fall into the trap of being so busy helping your organization, charities, your family, and friends that there's little left over for yourself. That's not a sustainable way to live. A centered life is one where you give time to all its facets: emotional, intellectual, charitable, social, spiritual, and physical. If any one is ignored, you get off balance and can't be your best.

Aside from exercise, nutrition is a huge part of maintaining a healthy lifestyle. In our world today we are bombarded with nutritional information so none of us can plead ignorance about the value of different types of food. We are killing ourselves with the food choices most of us make. Fatty, processed foods filled with chemicals—it's no wonder our medical costs are so high. When

I eliminated processed foods from my diet, my energy level soared. This is not an extreme measure; you just make it a habit to eat food that isn't processed. It saves time in the grocery store because you can eliminate many aisles. Vegetables, meats, fruit, and dairy products are all fresh foods that can be prepared easily. Read the label, and if there's a listing of ingredients that you have never heard of, or can't pronounce, don't buy it.

Leadership takes discipline and good habits, and both are manifested in what we eat and how often we exercise. The straightforward leaders I have observed are people who have developed consistently good habits in their personal lives. They are people of moderation who stick to a routine that keeps them performing at a peak level, which in turn is projected in their professional life.

"The body and mind are one."

Another aspect to a centered life are the boundaries you create to protect your privacy. We live in a world of too much information about everyone. Do you really want the leader of your organization to have a personal life that everyone knows about and discusses? Maintaining privacy demonstrates that you respect yourself and those close to you.

When I speak to younger audiences, they often are surprised that I entered public life at the age of 26. I encourage them to think about serving. I also warn them: if Facebook and digital cameras had existed when I was in college, I may not have been elected to office at age 26 because, like most college students, I would have had a Facebook page chronicling all of my good times in college. Those Internet postings don't show you in a well-rounded context.

Be careful how you use social media. It's an essential way to communicate, but invites indiscretion. It's too easy to post photos and make instant comments that you might later regret. A new company called Social Intelligence Corp. takes all the information you have provided on Facebook, Twitter, and LinkedIn, and supplies it to your prospective employer. Think about that before your next post. Make sure your Internet presence reflects your good works and accomplishments and a balanced picture of your life.

I never gave much thought to the issue of privacy until I lost my anonymity in the Tampa Bay media market when I became mayor. Tampa is the fourteenth largest media market in the country so I have to travel quite a distance to not be recognized. Here in my hometown, that loss of privacy is probably permanent. Once a mayor, always a mayor. I have gotten accustomed to it and the positive far outweighs any negative. Still, it is the loss of a valuable asset and most people fail to look at privacy this way.

Straightforward leaders understand boundaries and protect their privacy. The measured and thoughtful leader, who is a person of substance who can manage a crisis with a cool head, is not going to put information in the public domain that has the potential to reflect poorly on himself or his organization. The mother who is a role model to her children is not going to post embarrassing photos of herself on Facebook. This is a discipline that reflects a centered life.

Finally, part of being focused, well-rounded, and caring is treating people as you would want to be treated—the age-old Golden Rule. Every person is important, regardless of social or economic standing. Whether at work or beyond, how you treat people is a remarkably accurate barometer of leadership. You are the sum total of all your life experiences. You cross paths with literally thousands of people in your lifetime and those interactions reflect the respect you accord all people.

Have you ever been to a party, or worse, a networking event, when the person talking to you is also scoping out the room looking for that all important big-wig? Or, at least, someone they perceive to be more important than you. True leaders believe every person is important. Your life is lessened when a person is only significant to you because of their wealth, position, or ability to help you get ahead. When I am with an individual who treats people in the service industry poorly, I know he is not leadership material. Restaurant staff, taxi drivers, lawn maintenance workers, cleaners—I have seen them all treated in ways that I consider disrespectful, and the person who treats them that way is always diminished in my eyes.

I wrote earlier about the race riot at my junior high school. In the aftermath of the unrest, the county school district started a human relations board to work out the issues that caused it. I served on the board in ninth grade and the guidance counselor assigned to work with us was Gwen Lamar. We worked closely together for the entire school year and built a relationship of mutual respect. She is now Gwen Miller. For the eight years I served as mayor, Gwen served on the Tampa City Council. We often laughed about our shared past and how unbelievable it was that I ended up as mayor and she on council. In life, you never know when you might find yourself in a business or social relationship with that person from your past. Relationships evolve and mature. Having consistent, positive relations with people throughout your life is a good way to live.

Once done with a certain period of your life, you may think the people you interacted with are part of a past. You don't expect they will be part of your future, but they may. Life has a circular pattern to it. Gwen and I parted ways when I was in ninth grade, having formed a positive and trusting working relationship. Four decades later, it made our relationship in the city something of greater value to each of us.

"Look at every relationship as permanent."

Being focused, well-rounded, and caring is a way to live and lead that demonstrates you are a leader, regardless of your title or lack of same.

Believe in Yourself, Try New Things

Straightforward leaders believe in their capabilities and are willing to try new things. They are confident, but not arrogant. Having an inflated view of oneself is contrary to good leadership; it is important to be realistic about your strengths and limitations. Knowing yourself and believing in your capabilities allows you to accept increasingly responsible positions and stretch yourself. Sometimes the new mantle of leadership causes you to stumble, and that, too, is part of the learning process, as long as you stay humble, learn quickly from mistakes, readjust your strategies, and absorb new information rapidly

In 2009 Raheem Morris was selected as the head coach of the Tampa Bay Buccaneers. At age 33, he was the youngest head coach in the NFL. Passionate and motivating, he quickly learned from mistakes and changed his coaching strategy. Was he ready for the top job? In 2011, he told a reporter:

It doesn't matter how old you are, and it doesn't matter where you are in your career. You have no idea what this job is until you do it. No one is ready.

Though young, Morris had experience in the NFL at various coaching positions. The Buccaneer owners took a risk hiring him, but, more important, Morris was willing to take a risk on himself. He was unafraid of failure. When you believe in yourself, failure is not the worst fate. Never knowing how far your abilities will take you is considerably worse.

I had an early experience with taking risk and assessing my capabilities.

Back home in Tampa after college, I became active in local politics at a time of upheaval. Three of the five county commissioners had been arrested by the FBI in 1983 for taking bribes. The governor had to appoint a commissioner just to have a quorum for board meetings. Then the voters embraced a new county charter that expanded the commission from five to seven elected members. The 1984 election promised change at the county level as voters were fed up with scandal.

My father and I attended a candidate forum for the 1984 county commission elections and we both agreed it was a fairly uninspired event.

Then my dad turned to me and said ...

"Why aren't you running?" Well, there were many reasons not to run. I was only 25 years old, just a few years out of college, with scant work experience, and no money. My credentials were few. What I did have were people who had confidence in me. My father and my mother both thought I was capable. The conversation that started that night continued with my mentor, Fran, and other close friends who had confidence in me, too.

Sometimes, that's all it takes — people who believe in you, who cause you to believe in yourself. Sometimes only one person believing in you is all it takes.

A spirited grassroots campaign that operated out of my parents' home ensued. My mother worked tirelessly and my father lured volunteers by the dozens with his superior Italian cooking. Sometimes I thought people were more interested in the menu than in my platform. We walked, phoned, licked envelopes, and morphed into an energetic team. As I became more experienced, my confidence grew. "I can do this," I thought. Two weeks after my twenty-sixth birthday, I was sworn into office as a Hillsborough County Commissioner.

My greatest growth as a young adult occurred during that first race.

First, the confidence that others showed in me bolstered my confidence in myself. Sometimes I wonder why the voters thought such an inexperienced, young candidate should have a chance to serve in an important position. Possibly it was because I was so unlike the corrupt commissioners who had disgraced the very notion of public service. People want to be proud of their leaders. I may have been inexperienced, but look what their experience had brought to the county! The public's belief in my capabilities and the support and belief of so many supporters helped me to believe in myself.

Second, there is no substitute for hard work. The campaign worked seven days a week and was highly organized. We outworked every other candidate. I owed my victory to the hard work and commitment of my campaign volunteers.

Third, you must be positive. Positive was my mantra from the beginning and it has never changed. This has become a core part of my life, to govern in a positive way. Politics today is often an exercise in negativism, but I believe in running positive campaigns and governing in ways that bring people together.

Fourth, if you don't try, you won't get ahead. How many times have you passed up opportunities for one reason or another? You must place yourself in the arena and be unafraid of failure. The fear of failure is an interesting phenomenon. Many will not pursue opportunities or even their life dream because of it. Yet, what is the worst that can happen if you fail? You typically are no better or worse off because of it. By trying, win or lose, you learn much about yourself. Running at such a young age seemed implausible at first, but as I spent more time campaigning, I grew as a candidate. Soon, what seemed impossible became the possible.

I was just beginning to learn my leadership lessons. Along the way, since then, I have sometimes stumbled and fallen short of what I expected of myself. That happens when you take risks, try new things and stretch your capabilities. Throughout my professional life I have thought about the opportunity the voters gave me. They took a risk with me and I have never wanted to let them down. More important, I have always wanted to exceed their expectations.

"Jump on major opportunities— they're rare."

After two terms on the county commission I was elected as the county's Supervisor of Elections. The 2000 presidential election was a turning point in my career, increasing my profile in our community and the state. I appeared on many national television programs addressing the issues in the disputed contest. Residents in Hillsborough County were pleased that our community was not subject to ridicule and lawsuits as were many Florida counties. People started telling me, "You ought to run for mayor."

My earlier study of civil rights, during my pursuit of a master's degree in American history, led me to think about a position where I could make a greater difference. Though the mayor's office seemed the best place to help shape the community, I couldn't see how I could supervise the November 2002 election *and* implement the touch screen technology, which would be used for the first time, *and* run for mayor. The mayoral election was in March of 2003. In order to mount a campaign, I would have to resign as the supervisor in the latter part of 2002. The transition to the new technology had to go well. I had been very involved in election reform and was a strong proponent of the new technology, which was a big change from a punch card ballot. It didn't seem to me that I could do justice to both. So I opted out of the mayor's race.

I kept hearing, "This is the biggest mistake of your life."

Maybe so, but I did what I thought was right.

After the successful election in November—sometime around Thanksgiving—I started getting calls from people who told me I should still consider running for mayor. This seemed ludicrous. The election was only months away and there were already three major candidates in the race who had been campaigning for eight or nine months. Well-funded and well-known, each of the existing candidates was credible and organized. Though we had successfully implemented the touch screen voting system, it seemed too late to enter the race.

Undaunted, several supporters commissioned a poll that showed I would be the front-runner. I was surprised. Still, with December and the holidays looming, my inclination was to pass on the opportunity. My ambivalence had two sources. One, the effect of being mayor on my family. Our children were in middle school and being mayor meant placing our family in a spotlight. Two, resigning as supervisor of elections was final—no going back. It was a risk, something I could not treat lightly. My husband, Mark, wasn't eager for me to run. His natural inclination is to be protective of me and he was concerned about starting the campaign so late in the game.

Then something turned the tide. I received a phone call in mid-December from a person whom I've known for years — somebody I respected. I suppose his call was well-meaning, but the effect it had on me was the opposite of what he intended. He cautioned me not to run, saying the race had already been decided. One candidate, who he indicated was supported by the Tampa power structure, had the money and the connections. The caller suggested I would be badly beaten if I entered the race, and my political career would be over.

Time to believe in yourself!

Sometimes it takes a moment such as this to crystallize your path. Being told I didn't have a chance, that the election had already been decided, was a jolt. Imagine telling a supervisor of elections that an election has already been decided before anyone had a chance to vote! His comments solidified in me the view that leadership begins with believing in yourself. I shared the conversation with Mark. "I'm running," I said. He agreed despite his earlier misgivings, and was extremely supportive.

I entered the race on January 6, 2003, and the election was in March — only 60 days away. The March election ended in a run-off. Two weeks later I won the race with 64 percent of the vote. I don't want to give the impression that winning was easy. I had my share of setbacks. Upon entering the race, Fran and I made a list of 20 business and civic leaders in the community I should visit to ask for their support. Dutifully, I paid a visit to each one. All 20 turned me down because they had already pledged their support to another candidate.

Feeling slightly rejected, I went back to Fran and asked, "Any more great ideas?" The reality was that my race for mayor wasn't going to be based on the support of those 20 individuals. It would be decided by the tens of thousands of voters in the city who were going to wait until Election Day to make their decision.

Even the most successful leaders are turned down, suffer set-backs, experience failure. It is part of life. Straightforward leaders always take these setbacks as an opportunity to learn, readjust, and get better. You have to keep going and it starts with believing in yourself and your abilities.

It is difficult to start a new business, change jobs, or take risks. When I ran for the county commission, what did I have to lose? Not much. I was single, not in a relationship, accountable only to myself. Later in life, with more responsibilities, the risks become greater. In the end, however, if you take no risks, you will not fulfill your dreams and aspirations. Think about the sheer act of having children—plenty of risk. From the moment of their birth it's a life-time of worry and concern about their safety and future. Yet people do it all the time. If you are constantly so risk averse that you won't step out of your comfort zone every once in a while, you likely won't fulfill your potential. After eight years as mayor I am glad I didn't listen to the naysayers. I'm glad I took the risk and was able to believe in my capabilities at the right time.

Throughout my life I have had opportunities arise simply be-cause I talk to people. Being willing to engage in new situations and being curious about the world around you leads to new discoveries. It's all part of the willingness to try new things. I find that leaders say yes, more than they say no, to new ideas and concepts.

Once, when I studied abroad in London, England for a col-lege semester, I found myself meeting the Prime Minister, Margaret Thatcher, due to an unlikely set of circumstances. I was walking past Number 10 Downing Street, the home of the Prime Minister. There was a large crowd of people craning their necks and jockey-ing for better positions along the rope line. Two elderly women—one wearing bright blue and the other in bright pink—walked right past the guards and were ushered into the residence. They were quite noticeable and I wondered who they were—government of-ficials or dignitaries. They certainly didn't look very official. Several hours later, I saw those same two women near Westminster Abbey. I walked up to them and asked, "Aren't you the two women I saw entering the Prime Minister's home?"

"Oh, yes," they replied. "We're her friends."

We talked for several minutes. I shared with them my interest in politics and the details of my semester abroad. They couldn't have been nicer. These two women had helped Prime Minister Thatcher when she began her political career. They asked if I wanted to meet her. "Well, of course I'd like to meet her!" I said. They asked where I was staying, but I didn't expect anything to happen. Much to my surprise I received a beautiful handwritten note a few weeks later inviting me to a reception for Prime Minister Thatcher in Finchley. I attended and met the Prime Minister and her husband, Denis. Mrs. Thatcher had intense blue eyes and she looked at me directly, unwaveringly. She seemed interested in my studies. The attention Mrs. Thatcher afforded me is a trait I have observed in successful people. She treated every person as important.

Already drawn to politics, the encounter created even greater enthusiasm. I have never forgotten the importance of paying attention to young people. When I became mayor I started a Mayor's Youth Corps that promoted civic involvement for high school students. Your encounter with a young person could spark an interest, and even change the direction of his life. Be kind, sincere, and engaged. This is a form of mentoring and its positive influence should not be taken lightly.

If you want extraordinary things to happen, be engaged. Participate in the world around you. Meet new people, ask questions, and attend new events. You never know whom you will meet and what new opportunities will unfold.

"Be engaged in the world outside."

A centered life involves measured risks based upon your capabilities. You have to believe in yourself, stretch to get to the next level, try new things and relish the world around you. Only through trial and error can you actually determine your true strengths and weaknesses. The leader is often asking others to act in those ways. You have to first show that's how you live your life.

Create Balance Between Home and Work

I'll never forget bringing my daughter Caitlin, our firstborn, home from the hospital. Seven pounds, thirteen ounces, all swaddled in a pretty pink blanket. Carefully I walked into the house and laid her down in her new crib. Then I wondered, "What do I do now?" I had read all the books, gotten advice from all quarters. But really, what do you do with a newborn? I was now responsible for the health, safety, and development of another human being! What if I wasn't any good at it? What if I made a mistake? So begins the great adventure called parenting. Filled with unknowns, it comes without a manual and you often have to rely on instincts. It has been the most meaningful part of my life.

How do you live a centered life when you are faced with raising your children and working outside the home or working from home? You are pulled in many different directions which can leave you wondering how you can excel at all of them. This issue of balance has bedeviled women and men since women entered the workforce. It is the one question I have been asked more than any other in my years of public service. There is no one good answer to how you raise your children and work full-time. Every experience is different. Somehow we get it done. My story may help you think about what's right for you and your family.

My husband and I met while I served on the county commission. Mark and I instantly knew we were right for one another and were married in 1987. I gave birth to Caitlin and, eighteen months later, to Graham during my time as county commissioner. In many respects becoming a mom made me less ambitious. Climbing the political career ladder seemed less important than raising our two children. From the moment I became a mother my life changed for the better. I enjoyed being with my family more than anything.

In those early years I was also tired. Graham didn't sleep through the night for three years! Although I had a lot of help, I was exhausted most of the time. My mother-in-law came over every day and stayed at our home and watched the children while we were at work. She cared for them with a great deal of love and attention. My parents would come over in the evening if we had an event to attend. I was fortunate.

With my two terms on the county commission coming to an end, I had to decide what career path to pursue. Most people suggested I seek a seat in the Florida Legislature and position myself to run for the United States Congress. This was very unappealing to me since I had two young children at home. I didn't want to be away from them, flying all over the state or country, having to be out most nights. I wanted to be home at the end of the day and read to them before bedtime.

I decided to run for the office of Supervisor of Elections. It was a local constitutional office; it had a meaningful purpose and didn't involve the rough-and-tumble of politics which can cause constant tension. When I announced my intentions, many political pundits declared my political career to be over. Some joked that the supervisor of elections office was so low profile it was like entering the federal witness protection program. Why wasn't I running for a more high-profile political position? The answer seemed pretty simple to me — I wanted to spend time with my children. The position was challenging and took a great deal of time, but it also gave me a certain degree of flexibility. I never regretted the decision.

My ambivalence about running for mayor had a lot to do with the possible effect on our children. After being elected mayor, there were many days when I wondered if I had made the right decision. Caitlin had just started high school and Graham was in middle school. Those are not easy years. I think there were many times when they were embarrassed to be seen with me. At that age, children don't want to be different. They all dress alike, talk alike, and act alike. Having your mom as the mayor makes you different. That's not always a positive in their young eyes.

Together we got through it. Today my children are full of pride in my work as a public servant. I don't see in them any signs of neglect. Despite the take-out dinners and my crazy schedule, they are well-adjusted, positive young adults and my husband and I are proud of them. Throughout all my years of public service I wanted them to see meaningful work being accomplished, whether it was counting votes, going back to school, or running the city. I hoped they would see how each person can make the world a better place.

How do you find the proper balance between work and raising your family? Start by not being so hard on yourself. This advice is for both mothers and fathers, although I see this trait more in women. We are constantly saying "yes" to everything, trying so hard to achieve in every single area, and then feeling inadequate. I decided early on that there were many things I couldn't do. I would never be the homeroom mom or chaperone field trips. I could rarely greet my children when they got off the bus.

But there was plenty I could do. I could pack my children's lunch and put a note inside, review all of their important papers and make a big deal over every grade and beautiful piece of handmade art. I could attend school functions and cheer them on at their athletic events. And I was home at night and could read to them before bedtime.

In other words, none of us can do it all. But why not focus on the things you can do? Don't overload your plate and then wonder why things start falling off the edges. Say "yes" only to what you can manage and then don't feel guilty. Keep in mind that your children really remember only one thing—how much you love them. They remember the feeling of love and security. You can provide that in many ways and it doesn't mean you have to stay up late making cupcakes for a school function.

My husband and I often laugh at how few memories our children have before the age of eight. Remember the time we took you to Disney World for three days? No. Remember the trip to North Carolina and fishing at the trout farm? No. Sometimes we wonder—what do they remember? We could have saved a lot of money. They remember family traditions and certain stuffed animals and squirting the butter onto the tub of popcorn at the movies. They remember hiding in a cardboard box that the new refrigerator came in and the time they fell off a bike. They remember their grandfather cooking some special Italian meal he named after them, their dad throwing them in the pool, and me spraying them with the garden hose as they ran around the front lawn. They remember simple moments of family life. There is no need to go all out to create family memories. A happy, stable home life is the best memory.

The challenge is in having a happy, secure home life. Whether you are married, in a committed partnership, or a single parent, children need consistency and love. Then it extends to your life outside of your home. Is your job fulfilling? Does it give you enough flexibility so you can attend a function at your child's school or take your child to the doctor? Is your commute a nightmare? Do you feel that your work is meaningful?

I see many frazzled women who feel that daily life is one giant stress ball. They feel inadequate as mothers because they aren't the homeroom mom, and they feel inadequate at work because they have told the boss that they can't work overtime. They stress about daycare, work, and home. Not a good way to live!

I wrote earlier about embracing your reality. I suppose some people don't want to embrace their reality because they don't like their reality. Changing your reality usually doesn't happen overnight. It often takes long-term planning. This is where having a strategic plan for your life comes into play. One of the good things about living in America in the 21st Century is the vast array of choices we have. Your alternatives expand with more education and training. Only you can evaluate all of your options and create a reality that you can embrace.

If you work outside the home and are raising children ask yourself, do I have a job or a career? A job is something you do just to earn money to support your family. A career offers greater fulfillment and should be a passion. You tend to feel stuck in a job. In a career you are charting your course for the long-term.

The best thing about a career is that it is long-term in nature. Your climb up the corporate ladder might take 20 years. You might move from sales to management over a 15-year time frame. You may go from starting as a realtor to owning your own brokerage in 10 years. Careers take long-term thinking and planning. They usually involve starting at an entry level position and working your way up. They involve education and training and continuous learning.

Now let's put children into the equation. In my case, I altered my career path. Instead of taking on a highly political position that was going to cast a long shadow over my personal life, I chose a political post that was quieter, more settled. Did I give up on my career in public service? No. I changed the course of my career. Ultimately, as mayor, I ended up in a high-profile political position with a lot of responsibility. I felt fulfilled professionally. So the fact that I slowed down my career, went down a less ambitious route for an interval, didn't affect my ultimate career success.

Take a good hard look at your career and decide how you can best balance your work with raising your children. Make sure your work doesn't diminish your family life to the point where your household becomes stressed and unhappy. All the toys and fancy vacations in the world can't compensate for a hectic and stress-filled home life. You will never feel right if you believe you are shortchanging your children and their needs. It will nag at you like a pebble stuck in your shoe.

Evaluate the long-term trajectory of your career. Is it possible to work part-time as an attorney and go back to full-time work when the children are older? Can you discuss with your boss a way you can travel less but still provide value to your company? Is this the time to take a hiatus from work and get the advanced degree that may help you progress in the workforce later? Or, do you want to transfer to another part of the company that has different responsibilities?

You might be reading this and thinking, what about fathers? I know many families where the husband stays at home while his wife works full-time outside the home. Over the years I have seen all kinds of situations work for individual families. Each family should evaluate the two incomes. Does one partner have a career and the other a job? Is one a passion and one a chore? Figure out which career is best for the family, regardless of who is in the position. Then make your decision as a team. Make it in a positive, rational way. It may very well be that it's the husband who scales back to spend more time with the children. Figure out what works for the family unit.

For all the change in our society on so many fronts, women still assume the primary caregiver role with their children. My husband has been a wonderful father, but he probably didn't know about the field trip on Friday or the gift for the teacher that was due on Monday. In our marriage I, like most women, took most of the responsibility for knowing the daily details of our children's lives even though I, too, had a full-time career.

This was true even when I was mayor. I packed the lunches, got the children off to school, and did all of the endless school paperwork. I did the grocery shopping and the laundry. I just added my mayoral duties on top of everything else. My brain was always divided in two parts, city business and children. At work I might be dealing with a big issue one minute, and in the next thinking about something one of my kids needed for a school project. I knew where they were and, most of the time, with whom. I went through all the trials and tribulations of their teenage years while I was mayor. In fact, being mayor was easy compared to being a mother of two teenagers!

I was involved and the children knew it and probably wished I wasn't quite so involved. There were many evening events I didn't attend as mayor so we could have a good balance at home. In retrospect, I don't believe the citizens of Tampa suffered because I skipped some social functions.

We all have to make judgment calls about our home lives. Find the fit that's right for you. Don't let other people tell you how to live your life or make you feel guilty about your decisions. Don't take on more than you can handle. Stop saying "yes" to everything! Have faith in yourself to make the right decision. There is no one right way of doing things—but you will know when your lifestyle feels right.

> "Feel good about what you can do."

In the end, your children want to see a happy mother or father, a happy family. They care less about material things than they do about emotional attention. You give off a vibe and you want that vibe to be balanced and calm. Take stock of your life and make the necessary changes so you can feel good about both home life and work.

The Path to Straightforward Leadership: Step 5—A Centered Life

In this chapter, we have examined the importance of a centered life, where certain habits and practices show you to be a leader, regardless of position or title. A centered life means you:

- Are focused and can create positive paths forward when faced with challenges
- Set an example by taking care of yourself, and by setting boundaries to protect your privacy

- Treat every person well
- Have the confidence to try new things and take risks and
- Strike the right balance between home and work

Leadership is the act of guiding others to improve. Stop and recognize the leadership that is within you. Give yourself credit for wearing the mantle of leadership even though you may not be in the workforce. Use those talents you possess to do even greater good. Our world needs straightforward leaders.

CONCLUSION

—◈—

S TRAIGHTFORWARD LEADERS, WHO FIRST LEAD themselves and then effectively lead their organizations, will make a much needed contribution to society. The leadership problem we face as a nation, in business, government, and community requires an infusion of talent, of people committed to a mission larger than their own personal advancement or enrichment. Our Founding Fathers weren't perfect; they made many mistakes, but when the times called for them to step up and change the course of history, they did it without regard to their own personal popularity, financial status, or political ambitions.

They showed real leadership plain and simple. They were able to do it because they had developed the characteristics discussed throughout this book. In addition, they had acquired a broader perspective on the world that went beyond their colonial borders, and they understood the inevitability of change, and, because they lived centered lives, they were able to work toward goals much bigger than their own personal desires. They also understood the importance of finding the middle ground, they believed in compromise, and they tried to understand all points of view. Our Founding Fathers didn't wait for someone to ask them to lead. When the times called for leadership, they were ready. We have benefited from their courage and straightforward leadership for centuries. It is time for that style to emerge again.

Though we suffer from a leadership deficit, there is cause for hope. As a nation, we have long had the ability to change course, re-invent business and government, and step up and meet our challenges. Americans are resilient. While we live in problematic times, they are not nearly as challenging as times in our country's past.

The period following the Civil War clearly demonstrates that resilience in the face of overwhelming challenges. The best book on this subject is *April 1865* by Jay Winik,[9] who describes this tumultuous month in which President Lincoln was assassinated and the Civil War ended. The war took an unbelievable toll on our nation. Over 620,000 died. Thousands more were wounded and returned home to shattered economies in both the North and the South. There was great bitterness on both sides, and, unfortunately for the country, the tone set by President Andrew Johnson lacked the conciliatory approach favored by Lincoln. Slaves were free, but had few opportunities to support themselves. The nation was in a precarious state.

Looking back, one wonders how we came together, how we came to see our way forward to rebuild and emerge stronger. From the wreckage of the Civil War came a new nation, one no longer separated by slave states and Free states. Winik points out that we became a "new America, reunited, yes, scarred, certainly, but for the first time, largely whole, looking as much to the future as to the past."

---

9. Jay Winik, *April 1865: The Month That Saved America*, New York: HarperCollins, 2001.

And what did that future hold for our country? Constant progress. The Industrial Revolution. The growth of business giants. In the decades that followed the names Ford, Sears, Edison, Bell, Woolworth, Campbell, Rockefeller, and Carnegie became synonymous with America's new role. A little over one hundred years after the Civil War ended, our nation became the world's superpower. We progressed and changed, and, slowly, became a nation of opportunity. From the smoldering ruins of war, we remade ourselves and became stronger as one nation.

We can solve today's issues, but we need to change our approach. We cannot expect that "one" leader to solve our problems. This is an unrealistic view of what is going on in our country; it is also an unhealthy way to look at the current deficit in leadership which pervades business as well as government. Rather, it will take all of us to solve the problems that we face as a nation. We *all* have within us the ability to grow as leaders. If you discipline yourself to practice the qualities, traits, characteristics, and competencies of the straightforward leader, you can become an integral part of making your family, your community, and your organization stronger. In doing so, our country becomes stronger.

Straightforward leaders are needed. There are serious problems to be solved, organizations and institutions to be improved, and change to be implemented. It starts with you.

INDEX

—◊◊◊—

147